HOW TO HAVE A
BRILLIANT
LIFE

Prentice Hall LIFE

If life is what you make it, then making it better starts here.

What we learn today can change our lives tomorrow. It can change our goals or change our minds; open up new opportunities or simply inspire us to make a difference. That's why we have created a new breed of books that do more to help you make more of *your* life.

Whether you want more confidence or less stress, a new skill or a different perspective, we've designed *Prentice Hall Life* books to help you to make a change for the better. Together with our authors we share a commitment to bring you the brightest ideas and best ways to manage your life, work and wealth.

In these pages we hope you'll find the ideas you need for the life *you* want. Go on, help yourself.

It's what you make it

* * *

**Second
Edition**

HOW TO HAVE A
BRILLIANT
LIFE

Put a little bit more in
Get so much more out

MICHAEL HEPPELL

**Prentice Hall Life
is an imprint of**

Harlow, England • London • New York • Boston • San Francisco • Toronto
Sydney • Tokyo • Singapore • Hong Kong • Seoul • Taipei • New Delhi
Cape Town • Madrid • Mexico City • Amsterdam • Munich • Paris • Milan

PEARSON EDUCATION LIMITED

Edinburgh Gate
Harlow CM20 2JE
Tel: +44 (0)1279 623623
Fax: +44 (0)1279 431059
Website: www.pearson.com/uk

First published in Great Britain as *Brilliant Life* in 2008
Second edition published 2012

© Hadrian Holdings 2008
© Gloop Up 2012

Pearson Education is not responsible for the content of third-party internet
sites.

ISBN: 978-0-273-76122-8

British Library Cataloguing-in-Publication Data
A catalogue record for this book is available from the British Library

Library of Congress Cataloging-in-Publication Data
Heppell, Michael.
  How to have a brilliant life : put a little bit more in, get so much more out
  / Michael Heppell. -- 2nd ed.
     p. cm.
  Previously published under title: Briliant life.
  ISBN 978-0-273-76122-8 (pbk.)
  1. Self-actualization (Psychology) 2. Success. 3. Self-help techniques.
  I. Title.
  BF637.S4H465 2012
  158--dc23
                        2011033606

10 9 8 7 6 5 4 3 2 1
15 14 13 12 11

Design by Design Deluxe
Typeset in Helvetica LT Std 9/12pt by 3
Printed in Great Britain by Henry Ling Ltd, at the Dorset Press, Dorchester,
Dorset

This book is dedicated to Christine

Brilliant Wife = Brilliant Life

CONTENTS

PART 7 YOUR CAREER 213

PART 8 YOUR PERSONAL DEVELOPMENT 257

ABOUT THE AUTHOR

MICHAEL HEPPELL is one of the top professional speakers in the world, a bestselling author and an extraordinary trainer who works with top companies, sports professionals and high-performance individuals who all want to have brilliance in their lives.

He works across the world, influencing powerful changes in people and inspiring them to become brilliant at whatever they choose. He's helped companies to make billions, schools and colleges to raise levels of achievement, coached the best to be even better and through his books and seminars has helped thousands of individuals achieve their goals.

Through the Michael & Christine Heppell Fund and various community projects, Michael works with numerous community groups, charities and individuals helping at-risk people to change their lives in positive ways.

Michael lives in Northumberland, England, with his wife Christine and their family.

ACKNOWLEDGEMENTS

First of all, I must thank my business partner, co author, proof-reader, creative genius, most fearsome critic, mother of my children and love of my life; Christine, you are my Brilliant Life. Also big love and a huge thank you to my Brilliant Children, Michael and Sarah, for your patience during this project and your input which I know you'll read and say 'That was my idea!' Your contribution is noted, as is the request for a percentage of the royalties! A massive healthy thank you to Dr Fiona Ellis for her input and inspiration with the health section of this book – you are amazing; I could not have done it without you. Thank you to the Brilliant Team at Pearson who manage to take my ramblings and turn them into Brilliant Books. Rachael Stock, my editor for *How to Have a Brilliant Life*, who inspires me to raise my game with brutal honesty and total encouragement in just the right amounts. The production, admin, marketing and salespeople at Pearson – you are all so passionate about what you do and it shines. Thank you to Michael Foster at The Rights House for total faith (it's coming) and Annabel Merullo for making me worth more. Thank you to all the other contributors whom I interviewed, bamboozled and 'knowledge fished' for extra information: Salvatore LaSpada, George Hepburn, Peter Field, Simon Woodroffe and countless others. I have a fabulous team at Michael Heppell Ltd who make my life easier every day. Vanessa, Ruth, Ali and Sheila an extra special thank you to you for getting Christine and I to where we need to be, building amazing loyalty with our clients to the point where they always make a point of telling us how fabulous you are and ensuring that it's always a Brilliant Day at Michael Heppell. Thank you to Laura who keeps the ship shipshape even when the captain is pacing the deck. Welcome to the new people who have come into my life over the last year or so who support so strongly what we do: Peter and Sally, Glyn and Kay, Fi and Alun, Collette, Davina and Matthew, Sarah C and Fat Tony. Thank you to all my followers on twitter (I'm **@michaelheppell**) and to all my facebook friends (**facebook.com/michaelheppellofficial**) for getting involved. To our favourite clients (even though we know we shouldn't have favourites) Steve, Fiona, Sarah and Paul; Alistair, Stephen and Gemma thank you for having faith in us and making work such fun. For technical wizardry Norman and Neil at Datawright, Justin at the team at Carrot Media you are the greatest geeks. Jonathan Raggett and the amazing people at Red Carnation Hotels you make our time away from home our home from home – you are the best in the world for a reason, thank you for being suppliers, clients and above all friends. A tuneful thank you to Philip Ball who has created the soundtrack to our lives. And to all my old friends and family (you know who you are), thank you for sticking by me. Thank you to God for giving me the gift of being able to speak with confidence, write at will and entertain daily. Thank you to all the booksellers who choose to stock this book: writing a book means nothing without the brilliant people who sell it. And finally thank you to you for being interested enough in creating your own Brilliant Life that you now own your very own copy.

INTRODUCTION

Most people leave their quality of life to chance – big mistake!

Here's a challenge. Stand with your legs slightly apart. How do you feel? If someone was to give you a shove, I bet you could stay exactly where you are – easy.

Now stand on one leg. A little wobbly? Perhaps, but you'll quickly adjust and find your balance.

Finally, as you stand, put your head back, close your eyes and lift one leg from the floor. This time you'll be lucky to stay up straight for more than a few seconds. Hopping helps, as does waving your arms around, but the fact remains it's tough to get a balance with your eyes closed standing on one leg. But that's what you do every day with real life. It's tough... blinding... and full of wobbles.

So what's the solution? It is common these days for people to talk about achieving the elusive 'work/life balance'. I can't help thinking this implies that if you try to be brilliant in one area of your life then other parts suffer so you need to 'balance' things out. This has always seemed crazy to me as I would argue that you can have a brilliant life in all aspects so long as you open your eyes, plant your feet firmly where they should be and know how to work each part to ensure that you get the results you really deserve.

This book shows you how to do that, and in simple steps. Using a powerful tool called the Wheel of Life, you will soon identify which areas of your life need some attention right now and which areas you are doing well in. This will enable you to focus your energy and valuable time on specific parts of your life, those where it's most needed.

And here's the exciting part – it's not difficult. In fact, creating a brilliant life is easy when you know how. And the know-how is all right here. This book is your own personal guide to living a brilliant life. One that gives you the most satisfaction, the most happiness, the most achievement, the most feelgood moments and the most fulfilment.

The way we're going to do it is to break down your whole huge, complex life into key areas, such as work, family, money and health. You won't want to work on absolutely everything at once, and so I'm going to help you give yourself a simple score on each area, to see where it is you need to focus your attentions first (the lowest scores are where simple actions will make the biggest difference to your life – and fast). We'll then break down each area into smaller chunks to again give you the chance to identify and improve the areas where you personally need most help. The techniques I'm going to share with you are a distillation of the very best tips, tools and techniques – the stuff that when whittled down to the barest essentials, really makes the biggest difference. They are in the main simple – some will give you a very quick result, others will need more effort (always worthwhile in order to get the best results). By taking the time to start now, you will soon be living a Brilliant Life.

How to get the most out of this book

When I started to study personal development and self-improvement, I found myself using lots of different tools and techniques and testing each one for a short period of time before making up my mind whether or not this was going to be a part of my life. The fact is some of the ideas I learned actually contradicted each other but, rather than making an instant decision about what was right or wrong, I would test out the different tools and techniques first. Then and only after applying them for a few days, weeks or months, would I make my own mind up. May I suggest you do the same as you read *How to Have a Brilliant Life*? Don't discard any of the ideas until you've tested them out in your own life first. What may not work for one person may work brilliantly for you.

The ground rules

It is essential to read and work through Chapter 1 in its entirety – this will give you the foundations. Thereafter you can jump around from chapter to chapter or heading to heading, deciding which area you need to work on next. The good news is that you may only need to read half of the book to see the biggest improvements in your life, right now.

How to Have a Brilliant Life is designed to be a guidebook to life that you can use now and many times in the future. You will discover that chapters that seem irrelevant to you now will become important later. Life's like that too. Read the parts you need to read now, and turn to the rest as and when you need them.

As you're working on a very important project – your life – you may want to keep both a pen and highlighter nearby as you read through the sections. Certain sections will jump out at you – highlight these and jot your own thoughts in the margin. Use this book as a workbook – not simply something you read. By doing this, you will get so much more from every page and be able to review your progress in the future.

And, finally, *don't lend this book to anyone*. Normally, I'm a big fan of sharing knowledge, but this is going to be a private journey just for you. There will be lots of personal information in this book from the things you've worked through and the notes you've made, so I imagine you'll want to keep this safe.

Are you ready? Then let's begin. Here's to your Brilliant Life!

MICHAEL HEPPELL

THE WHEEL OF LIFE

Let's get you started straight away. You'll need a pen and a few minutes as you're about to complete your first Wheel of Life. This simple tool will allow you measure how well you are doing in all the key areas of life. Your wheel will change each time you complete it, so this is a snapshot in time, and your starting point towards that elusive Brilliant Life. This first wheel is going to form the basis of how you read the rest of this book, so take a few minutes to complete it with your full attention. I'll give you full instructions plus some hints and tips to help you to get the best out of the process.

You'll notice the wheel is split into eight key areas and we'll look at every one in more detail later in this book. Right now all you are going to do is give yourself a simple mark out of 10 for how well you think you are doing in each.

Here are a few helpful hints to ensure you get the most from completing your first wheel:

★ BE HONEST! It's easy to fill in the wheel and cheat a little by adding one or two marks to your scores. But, at the end of the day, who are you really cheating?

★ Don't dwell. Your first wheel is a snapshot so you don't need to spend a long time thinking about each area. You'll have time to do that later when you go into more detail during the following chapters.

★ Avoid half marks. By that I mean if you feel like you are wavering between a 5 or a 6 give yourself a 5 and move on.

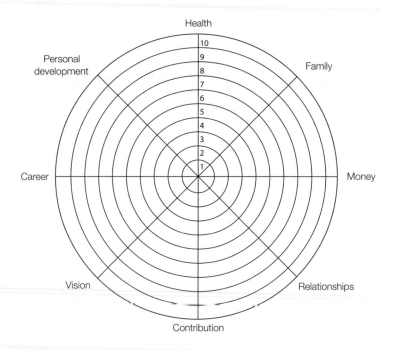

Read each of the following descriptions on your wheel and give yourself an honest mark out of 10. Zero is low. It doesn't get any worse. Ten is high which means perfect, it doesn't get any better. You may find yourself somewhere in between.

Your health

Do you jump out of bed feeling amazing or do you need to press the 'snooze' button several times before you drag yourself from under the duvet and into the shower? Do you look in the mirror and say 'wow' or do you avoid your reflection thinking 'woah'? Do you have an abundance of mental energy or do you feel yourself getting frustrated and stressed? And how's your diet? You know what you should be eating and drinking but how well are you doing?

If you're the picture of health then it's a high mark here. Overweight, lacking energy, body niggles, unhappy with health or just 'not yourself' then it's a lower mark. Give yourself an honest mark out of 10 for your health.

Your family

Is your family unit tight and are all your relationships perfect? Or are you happy with how you get on with some family members, but others you could happily never see again? If your family life is working well and you feel that you are full of love and caring then you get high marks. If not then consider the mark you need to give. Even if some areas are great but others aren't so good then average out where you stand and give yourself a mark for family.

Your money

Are you a whizz with money and right up to date with all financial knowledge? Do you invest, know the difference between good and bad credit, and are you comfortable with your financial state? Well done; high marks. Or are you the type of person who has too much month at the end of their money? Do you find yourself fretting over finance and worrying unnecessarily about money? If so, that's a low mark, I'm afraid. Give yourself a score.

Your relationships

How well do you get on with others? What are your relationships like with your colleagues, your boss, your neighbours? This is your chance to measure your relationships with everyone you come in contact with or know. That's a lot of people, so be honest and give a score based on how you feel generally. Are you the life and soul of the party, the one who remembers important details about people and the one who can be relied on to keep a secret? Or is your idea of strictest confidence only telling others one at a time? Score yourself now for how well you think you're doing with relationships.

Your contribution

How much time do you give to help others? Are you committed to going the extra mile without the need for recognition or reward? If you're a person who is conscious of the impact you make on the world around you and is actively making a difference then it's high marks here. If you would like to do more if you had more time, then I'm sorry, you don't get marks for what you would like to do, you get marks for doing it. Be honest and give yourself a score for your contribution.

Your vision

Do you know where you will be and what you will be doing in the next 5, 10 or 20 years? Do you have your goals set, written down and with a plan on how you will achieve them? Or is your nearest thing to a written goal your daily 'to do' list? Is the idea of a 10-year plan scary because you don't even know what you are going to be doing next week? You know how this works now so give yourself an honest mark for your personal vision.

Your career

Do you jump out of bed on a Monday morning and think 'Work – yippee! I love it so much I'd do it for free!' Are you in the job of your dreams with amazing rewards and a career plan all laid out so you know exactly where you are going? Well done, it's high marks for you. Or do you simply go to work to pay the bills? Is the idea of an exciting career something from the dim and distant past? If your career isn't all that great then give yourself an honest mark to reflect that. Score where you are for career right now.

Your personal development

When did you stop learning? Or are you still a glutton for education? What are you doing right now for your own personal development?

How much of your time are you investing in making you better? If you're reading the right books, working with mentors and spending time on you then it's high marks here. Be honest with this one; it's one of the most important sections of your Wheel of Life.

Once you have scored all eight sections take a moment to join up your scores. *See the example.*

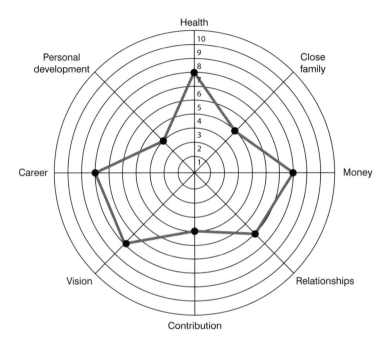

Take a look at your 'wheel'. Is it any wonder that life is a bumpy journey? The good news is that you are about to tackle the challenging areas head on and with the dozens of ideas, tools and techniques in this book you'll soon have a brilliant and more balanced life.

Where to start?

Do you remember when you went to primary school and you used to play with scales? You probably worked out quite quickly that the heaviest weights had the biggest effects. The heaviest weights on your wheel are the areas with the lowest scores. So they are the ones we are going to tackle first.

Take a look at your wheel and, starting with the lowest score, make a list of your results:

1 (lowest score)

2

3

4

5

6

7

8 (highest score)

Now you've identified your strongest and weakest areas, you can simply jump to the part of the book that covers your weakest area. Giving this your full attention now will give you instant big results. When you've completed this one, and feel ready, move on to your second weakest and so on. This is the quickest and most effective way to make your life truly brilliant.

PART ONE
YOUR HEALTH

THE HEALTH
WHEEL

Welcome to the Health Wheel. I am indebted to my great friend and health mentor Dr Fiona Ellis of the Highfield Road Wellness Centre (**www.hrwc.co.uk**) for her invaluable input, help and advice for this section of the book.

You'll notice that the Wheel of Health is broken down into three main categories:

1 Eat well (Effective eating, Food awareness, Hydration).

2 Move well (Structure and posture, Physical exercise, Breathing).

3 Think well (Stress, Body image, Sleep and meditation).

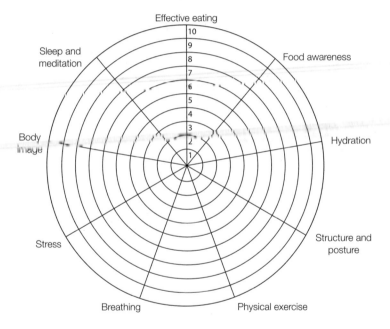

You're going to start by quickly rating yourself on each of these categories so you know where you're starting from. Then, on the assumption that there's room for improvement, you can turn to whichever chapter you think needs the most attention to find a host of simple, practical ideas to make your health better, starting today.

Eat well

Do you think about what you eat and drink, how you consume it and know what foods do what for your body? If you eat a wide range of nutritious healthy foods, take your time over eating and drink plenty of pure, unadulterated water, you'll score highly on this – maybe eight or nine.

If on the other hand you eat whatever is in front of you, no matter how packaged or polluted, if you usually eat 'on the go' and don't drink much apart from coffee and alcohol, you're at the other end of the scale. Only you can decide exactly where.

If you know the theory and generally have quite a good diet, but it tends to end up with ready meals in front of the TV a bit too often, you'll probably want to give yourself a middling mark.

Move well

Can you touch your toes? Do the heels of your shoes wear down unevenly? If you get out of breath after a short walk, feel a bit lopsided and realise when you think about it that you usually breathe fairly rapidly through your mouth not nose, then low marks here (something to build from!).

If you are as fit as a fiddle, both straight and flexible, and breathe deeply and through your nose into your belly, then top marks for you.

Good on some points but not so good on others, then choose to mark each spoke separately.

Think well

Stress is a big part of how you are mentally, but surprisingly you're not going to measure how much stress you have in your life; you'll measure how you think you deal with it.

Give yourself an honest mark for how well you think you manage stress, but also factor in how you feel about your body image, and your sleep patterns.

So, if you sail through a busy schedule with calm and ease, sleep a good, refreshing eight hours a night and think 'not bad' when you look in the mirror, and find it easy to switch off, then high marks.

If you often feel tense and overwhelmed, would rather not look in a mirror at all thank you very much and know you go to bed way too late and sleep fitfully, then very low marks here.

Good on stress but poor on sleep or any other good/bad combination, and you'll have a middling score for 'think well' – your mental well-being.

Adding it all up

Now join up the scores and you'll see quite quickly how well you are doing in the three big regions of health. Are you happy with your scores or is it time to do something about this, the most vital area of the Wheel of Life?

Wherever you've got a low score, turn now to the section on that subject on the following pages and commit to taking an action on each section. Do it now and keep on doing it. Without brilliant health how can your brilliant life happen?

Remember to take action on any area where you have a lower score first and by using the simple ideas found here you'll soon find yourself re-scoring with better marks and a healthier life.

Here are a few things you need to know before we start:

★ I am not a health expert.

★ I am not a fanatic. Don't become one yourself.

★ In most of this part, I'm passing on knowledge that I've picked up and used from people who know a lot more about health than I do.

★ Being healthy is a constant conscious process; what you learn here needs to be treated as a guide. Just keep on doing it!

EAT WELL

We live in busy times. Food 'on the go' is now seen as the norm and a family meal is becoming a thing of the past. However, we are more tuned in to 'reading the packaging' than ever before, but have you noticed that once people buy their food they give little thought to how they prepare or eat it?

By taking time to appreciate what you are eating you'll not only feel better when you're eating, but you'll find it easier to control your weight, you'll feel better after meals and your body will get more nutrition from what you have eaten.

Effective eating

★ Do you find time to prepare food effectively?

★ Do you eat only when you're hungry?

★ Do you really enjoy your meals?

★ Do you eat slowly and chew all of your food well?

Or...

★ Do you eat 'on the go' or in front of the television?

★ Do you find yourself wolfing your food down and feeling full or even bloated after your meal?

★ Do you try to lose weight with the latest fad foods or combinations?

Here are a few things to do and things to avoid.

THINGS TO DO

★ Have a tranquil mind at meal times.

★ Chew each mouthful slowly.

★ Think about the taste of each mouthful.

★ Use your tongue to taste food as you eat it.

★ Eat slowly – it's not a race.

★ Only eat when you are hungry.

THINGS TO AVOID

★ Watching TV when you eat – turn off the box!

★ The 'diet' mentality.

★ Drinking liquid with your meal – separate liquid intake from eating by 10 minutes.

★ Eating while stressed or tired – this inhibits digestion and creates fermentation (yuk).

★ Eating while you are ill.

★ Overeating – easy to write, easy to read, hard to do – especially when the food is fantastic. So just ask yourself as you are eating, 'Have I had enough?' Then listen to your body for the answer.

BRILL BIT

Use chopsticks when eating. This will force you into taking smaller bites and will help you to slow down when eating a meal.

Food awareness

Food can provide your body with nutrients that cleanse your cells and give you energy and vitality; or food can kill your cells, suck vitality from your life and drain your energy. Sounds dramatic, but it's true.

However, nutrition needn't be a minefield and with a little time and thought you can quickly turn things around. The great thing about improved nutrition is that you see the results very quickly too; even after just a few days or weeks you'll notice differences.

Learn from others

Okinawa is a small island just off the coast of Japan. Its inhabitants, the Okinawans, are described as the 'longest lived people on the planet' and boast more centenarians than any community in the world. And it's not just that they've reached a ripe old age either – they're fit, healthy and agile too.

I don't know about you, but I'm interested to know what they do and how they do it. Actually it's very simple. They eat well, listen to what nature is telling them and practise pretty much everything that is in this health section of *How to Have a Brilliant Life*.

The principles of healthy eating

If you found yourself with low marks for food awareness then these 13 principles of healthy eating should form the foundations of your new approach to food:

1 Eat consciously and remember to breathe while eating.

2 Make vegetables and fruit 60% of your daily food intake. The most important foods to eat are the green vegetables and their juices. Aim to have a vegetable juice daily and vegetables or a salad with every meal.

3 Eat fruit as a snack on an empty stomach. Separate it from other foods if possible due to the fact it digests so rapidly. Don't eat fruit late at night.

4 Eat and/or supplement essential fats and oils. Have a serving of flax oil every day. Avoid frying with oils and use the best-quality olive oil you can afford on your salad.

5 Discover sprouted seeds and beans. Sprouting soybeans, pumpkin seeds and aduki beans makes them incredibly rich in vitamin C and zinc, and they are also very high in protein. Sprouting is a fun activity to do at home too.

6 Eat at least four servings of fresh fish per week. Fish is rich in Omega 3 oils that are not only amazing for your heart but also for your mind.

7 Choose organic, locally produced meat, eat small portions, and don't have meat every day.

8 Eat whole grains. Avoid 'white' processed grains. Try new grains like spelt, buckwheat, quinoa and different forms of rice.

9 Watch your carbohydrate intake. Choose low GI options, e.g. sweet potato instead of normal potato, spelt pasta instead of white pasta.

10 Eat dairy products and processed meats sparingly.

11 Invest in organic foods wherever possible, and get a good-quality vegetable wash to remove pesticides and chemicals when organic isn't an option.

12 Learn to reduce or eliminate acid-forming foods in your diet. These include alcohol, caffeine and carbonated drinks.

13 Avoid smoking.

> **BRILL BIT**
>
> Have a go at eating all the colours of the rainbow when you eat vegetables. Be daring!

Hydration

Thirsty? Then you are already severely dehydrated. And a slightly more embarrassing question. What colour is your pee?

Water makes up more than half the weight of your body:

★ Your brain is 76% water.

★ Your lungs are 90% water.

★ Your blood is 84% water.

Without water, you would die in a few days. Every cell in your body depends on water for its very function.

Water serves as a lubricant; it forms the base of saliva and the fluids that surround your joints. Water regulates the body temperature. Cooling and heating is distributed through perspiration. If you are dehydrated, you will never be able to function with amazing vitality and energy.

Have I persuaded you to drink lots of water yet? No? Well, here's one more reason:

★ 90% of the world's population is chronically dehydrated.

Side-effects of dehydration

★ Stress.

★ Headaches.

★ Back pain.

★ Allergies.

★ Weight gain.

★ Inability to lose weight.

★ Asthma.

★ High blood pressure.

★ Alzheimer's disease.

★ An overly acidic body.

So how do you get so dehydrated?

Just through activities of daily living. The average day's loss of fluid is four litres, which is generally replaced by the fluids we drink and the food we eat. The most common cause of increased fluid loss is exercise and sweating. (I bet just for a second there you thought 'Brilliant, I'll stop exercising then!') The effects of even mild dehydration are decreased coordination, fatigue and impaired judgement.

Do you know if you are dehydrated?

★ A dry mouth is the last outward sign.

★ If you are thirsty it means your cells are already dehydrated.

★ A severely dehydrated body produces orange or dark-coloured urine.

★ A somewhat dehydrated body produces yellow urine.

★ A well-hydrated body produces colourless urine.

How much water do you need to drink?

★ As a general rule, you need to drink at least two litres of water every day – not all in one go! I'd suggest you sip water most of the day, but give your system a rest for an hour or so a couple of times a day.

★ You should take in another two litres of water a day in the form of water-dense foods (fruit and vegetables).

★ You should start sipping water as soon as you wake in the morning. Treat yourself to half a litre before you leave home. This is when you are the most toxic and dehydrated.

BRILL BIT

Water-rich foods should make up 70% of your diet. This will allow your body to cleanse itself. Failure to consume this percentage means you are clogging your body – not cleansing your body. Did you know a lettuce is 97% water?

Oh yes and just in case I didn't make it clear, I'm talking about water. Not flavoured stuff or fizzy drinks. Did you know to neutralise one can of a soft drink would take 32 glasses of water?

3

MOVE WELL

For the first seven years of my working life I was a roofer. For much of my time putting on the slates and tiles I was in a twisted position leaning to the right. For the first two years of my apprenticeship I carried everything the slaters needed up ladders on my shoulder.

What the heck was I thinking about!

It was only years later when I was plagued with back pain, headaches and with my wife and children pointing out how 'lopsided' I was that I decided to visit an osteopath. WOW! I'm now a raving fan. I go, my family go, my friends go, everyone goes and everyone whom I have recommended calls me and thanks me because it's an area of our health that we just don't think about enough.

Structure and posture

I didn't realise just how important posture is but it ranks right up at the top of the list when talking about good health. Posture is as important as eating properly, exercising and getting a good night's sleep.

Good posture ensures:

★ Your bones are properly aligned and your muscles, joints and ligaments can work as nature intended.

★ Your vital organs are in the right position and can function at peak efficiency.

★ Posture also helps contribute to the normal functioning of the nervous system.

Without good posture, you can't be fully physically fit. The good news is that almost everyone can avoid the problems caused by bad posture *and* you can make improvements at any age. Many people don't realise how much they need a strong structural support system until their bones have decayed, they have a bent and twisted spine, their muscles are weak and they are in a lot of pain.

The musculoskeletal system comprises about two-thirds of your body mass and its management uses up nearly 90% of your body's energy. It has some obvious functions:

1 It keeps you 'upright.'

2 It allows you to get from A to B.

3 It protects your internal organs.

It's important. And the most important part is the spine. Your spine (and its individual vertebrae) is of vital importance because it protects your nervous system. Think about your nervous system as the central processor of your body; it controls and co-ordinates every function. It's worth looking after.

Prevention is the key

As a society we have been educated to think preventatively about the health of our teeth and eyes, but little else, and especially not our spines.

Think about this. All the functions and processes of your body are controlled by your nervous system and, in turn, this system adapts you to the many changes occurring moment by moment in your environment, so without a healthy nervous system your body will cease to work correctly. Illness and degeneration may result.

Chiropractors and osteopaths are the experts at diagnosis and treatment of poor posture and musculoskeletal misalignment, which can compromise the proper function of your body. And don't worry, osteopathy and chiropractic are philosophies of health – not just bone cracking and muscle stretching! Osteopaths and chiropractors work with the structure of the body, recognising the imbalance of joint position or mobility. Through touch, massage, manipulation and stretching techniques, they can diagnose and treat people with many physical and emotional problems – not just twisted former roofers!

What's your posture like?

I'd recommend everyone should see an osteopath or a chiropractor, but if you're not sure ask yourself if any of the following sound familiar:

★ You get musculoskeletal aches or pains.

★ You get headaches.

★ Your energy is consistently low.

★ Your posture is misaligned.

To see if your posture is misaligned look at yourself in a full-length mirror and check the following:

1 Are your shoulders level?

2 Is your head straight and not tilted to the side?

3 Does your chin jut forward?

4 Are the spaces between your arms and your sides equal on both sides?

5 Are your hips level and not sloped to one side?

6 Are your ankles straight and not turned in or out?

7 Is your lower back slightly curved forward, not too flat or curved too much?

8 Is your hem line uneven?

9 Do you wear down your shoes unevenly?

Here's some simple advice from my osteopath, Fiona, to improve your posture:

1 Stand with your feet parallel (not turned out) about a hip's width apart. Bringing your feet parallel engages the muscles in the front of your thighs and keeps your hips, knees and ankles in proper alignment.

2 Stretch up through your body to the top of your head. As you do so feel your spine lengthen as you get taller.

3 Bring your pelvis to a neutral position. To find this neutral position, place your hands around your hips, then tuck your tailbone in slightly until your pelvis is directly over your thighs. Make sure there is no bend in your hip joints and there's less sway in your lower back. As you tuck your tailbone in, you should feel your abdominal muscles engage slightly.

4 Draw your shoulders back and relax them down, bringing your hands in line with the seams of your trousers.

5 Level your chin, keeping your head directly over the spot between your shoulders, not forward or back.

That's a perfect posture!

BRILL BIT

Set your rear-view mirror in the car slightly higher so you have to do a little stretch to see it. This will remind you to sit up straight while driving.

Physical exercise

'The hardest step is the first one out of the front door.'
(TIM, THE FIREMAN WHO LIVES IN MY VILLAGE)

I see Tim when I'm out running and he's super-fit. Built like how you'd imagine a firefighter to be built and he really shifts along the lanes. But that quote from Tim is the real key to physical exercise. Getting started. Some days he doesn't want to, some days (lots actually) I don't want to. There are lots of really good excuses. You know how it is: it's cold and wet, the dark nights are coming, there's a million things on your 'to do' list – 'I'll start tomorrow'. Does that sound like you?

Why regular exercise is a must

It reduces health risks of many conditions, including high blood pressure, obesity, type 2 diabetes, heart disease, strokes and certain types of cancer.

Along with a healthy diet, exercise can help you lose weight – and then keep it off.

It keeps your arteries clear. Exercise increases the concentration of 'good' cholesterol and decreases the concentration of 'bad' cholesterol.

▶

It helps you manage chronic conditions and can lower high blood pressure, control blood sugar and relieve chronic muscle pain.

It strengthens your heart. Your heart doesn't need to beat as quickly when it is stronger and a stronger heart also pumps blood more efficiently, which improves blood flow.

Exercise activates your immune system and helps keep away viral illnesses, making you less vulnerable to minor viral illness such as colds and flu.

It makes you happier. Exercise can help depression and reduce anxiety.

Exercise may make you tired in the short term, but over the long term you'll enjoy increased stamina and reduced fatigue. Hurrah!

And for anyone who is older than they once were it helps you stay active and independent as you progress in years by keeping your muscles strong, which can help you preserve mobility as you get older.

Exercise also helps keeps your mind sharp. Researchers say that regular exercise can reduce cognitive decline in seniors.

Anything is better than nothing

You don't have to start by putting your name down for the London Marathon 'because that will make me exercise'. Start with the simple regular things and after a few weeks you'll feel the difference.

Here are a few ideas to get you started:

★ Invest in a mini-trampoline and walk or jog on it while watching TV (no excuse for bad weather and you can burn up to 300 cal/hour).

★ Put on some music and dance around the house (burn up to 400 cal/hour).

★ Take the stairs at work instead of the lift.

★ Rather than cursing because there aren't any spaces at the front, park as far away from the shops as possible and walk.

★ Get off the couch on to the floor, act like a cat and do some spinal and total body stretching.

★ Lose your chair and sit on a fitness ball while you are working.

★ Find an exercise buddy or join a group – the Ramblers are great.

★ Go to dance lessons, or yoga or a badminton class – try things until you find something you really enjoy.

★ Play with your kids.

★ Learn about then apply anaerobic exercise techniques. Brilliant for busy people.

The key is to start and enjoy yourself. 'No pain – no gain' is not a helpful strategy when embarking on exercise. Be sensible and start off slowly but surely. No one ever continues doing anything for long if it hurts!

BRILL BIT

Play 'Beat the week'. The idea is that if you exercise four or more times in any given week you've beaten the week. Hooray! Three times or fewer and the week beats you. Booo! You do want to win, don't you?

Breathing

Just stop for a moment and think about how you breathe. Is it through your nose, mouth or both? Do you breathe into your upper chest or deeply down towards your belly?

Take an interest in your breathing

Why? It's very, very important! It is clear that optimal oxygenation of your cells through proper breathing, nutrition, fluid intake, exercise and stress management is absolutely necessary in order to maintain your health.

You breathe approximately 28,000 times a day. If your breaths are shallow, taken in through your mouth and confined to the upper parts of your lungs, your body gets a message that you're facing an emergency. This creates and releases stress hormones, which, over time, can cause many adverse effects in your body.

How to breathe

Correct breathing is the key to oxygenating your cells, so it's worthwhile knowing how to do it properly:

★ Breathe in through your nose.
★ Breathe into the lower part of your lungs – so your tummy sticks out (I call them 'Buddha breaths').
★ Breathe slowly.

Power breathing exercises

Take 10 breaths three times a day in the following ratio:

★ Inhale for the count of three.
★ Hold for the count of six.
★ Exhale for the count of five.

Remember to breathe in through your nose and out through your mouth.

BRILL BIT

Get outdoors. It has been shown conclusively that indoor air quality is worse than outdoor air quality. If you must be indoors, throw open the windows, even in winter!

THINK WELL

Managing stress is not about removing all the stress from your life, it's about how you deal with the stress that's an inevitable part of your life that's important. Brilliant people don't have stress-free lives, they are simply able to handle it in a healthy way.

Dealing with stress

What does 'poorly controlled' stress do to you? If you don't deal with it well, you're more open to:

★ fatigue and low energy
★ overeating and difficulty with weight loss
★ grogginess in the morning
★ lack of sex drive
★ reliance on caffeine, sugar or drugs
★ difficulty in sleeping
★ poor concentration and memory
★ recurrent infections due to a lowered immune system
★ depression
★ the onset of Alzheimer's disease
★ sore and stiff muscles and joints
★ degeneration of your physical system
★ cancer, heart disease, strokes, diabetes, etc.

So it's a must that you deal with stress and do so *brilliantly*.

Here are some ideas to help you deal with the stress in your life.

Laugh

It has been proved time and time again that laughter stimulates the immune system, stimulates breathing, which oxygenates the body and uses nearly every muscle of your body – which in turn keeps you looking great.

Laughter by its very nature invites us to look at things in a different light. Look for the funny side of (almost) every situation – and don't be afraid to have a really good laugh out loud.

Be optimistic

A study compiled by the Mayo Clinic over a 30-year period shows that subjects who were categorised as pessimistic had a 19% greater chance of dying early than those described as being optimists.

Now that's something to be optimistic about.

Have fun

Having fun reduces stress, which reduces the amount of adrenalin the body produces.

Relax

Listen to a relaxation CD, quieten your mind and learn how to meditate. By practising deep relaxation for 15 minutes three to four times a week, you will significantly reduce your levels of stress. I recommend 'White Island' relaxation available as a CD or download from **www.michaelheppell.com** as an easy way to get started.

Love and be loved

A study at the University of Miami on premature babies found that babies who were stroked regularly gained weight 49% faster than those babies of the same birth weight who were not stroked.

In fact babies who are not touched and cuddled, even if they are cared for physically, are at a greater risk of death. Doctors call it 'failure to thrive'.

Manage anger

People with hostile personalities have up to five times the death rate before the age of 50 than people who are less prone to these negative emotions.

In a study carried out at the University of North Carolina, 13,000 participants were asked a series of questions about their levels of anger, i.e. whether they were hot headed, whether they felt as though they wanted to hit someone when angry, etc.

Of those questioned, 8% were at the high end of the spectrum. In the six-year follow-up period, it was found they were three times more likely to have died suddenly than those ranked lowest.

Get support

Having someone to talk to is a very powerful medicine. Get it off your chest. Have a whinge about your job, the kids, life and then let it go. A good supportive friend or spouse will hear you out and then support you when you move on.

Studies show that married men live on average four years longer than single men. Companionship and shared interests add mental stimulation, which boosts your immune system.

BRILL BIT

Be a lover not a fighter.

Body image

A poor body image can affect how you think and feel about yourself. A poor body image can lead to emotional distress, low self-esteem, dangerous dieting, anxiety, depression and eating disorders.

With a positive body image, a person has a real perception of their size and shape and feels comfortable and proud about their body. With a negative body image, a person has a distorted perception of their shape and size, compares their body with others and feels shame, awkwardness and anxiety about their body.

Learn to love what you see in the mirror

When you look in the mirror, what do you focus on? Do you like what you see? We are all (men and women, young and old) under pressure to measure up to a certain social and cultural ideal of beauty, which can easily lead to a poor body self-image. By cleverly presenting an ideal shape that is difficult to achieve and maintain, the cosmetic and diet product industries are assured of success. Because once you start looking for perfection, you just can't stop.

So let's start with what you've got.

Celebrate and nourish your body

We all want to look our best, but a healthy body is not always linked to appearance. In fact, healthy bodies come in all shapes and sizes!

Developing and nurturing a positive body image and a healthy mental attitude is crucial to your happiness and wellness. There is a common misconception that you have to be very thin to be healthy. This can then cause people to do all sorts of unhealthy things to become very thin – eating an inadequate diet, smoking, pills, etc.

Your body is amazing. Start right away by treating it well. Get a massage, sign up for a treatment, nourish your skin, look after your nails, floss your teeth, dry body brush, have a facial, exfoliate, clean your tongue, have a colonic irrigation, relax in an Epsom Salts bath, massage your feet and condition your hair. Then, in the afternoon . . .

Love you, love your body

It's easier to feel more comfortable and do the right things for your 'new' body when you find things to like about the one you have now.

Essentials to developing healthy body image are the same as for overall wellness:

★ Eating healthily – promotes healthy skin and hair and strong bones.
★ Regular exercise – increases self-esteem, self-image and energy.
★ Plenty of rest – the key to stress management and masses of energy.

Some thoughts on dieting

Dieting does not work! If it did, it would not be one of the fastest-growing industries in the world (think about that one). Dieters spend billions on weight-loss programmes that have little long-term effect on their weight.

Did you know that, even if you remain on a diet programme, it is likely that you will regain one- to two-thirds of your lost weight within one year? And nearly all of your lost weight within five years?

Women in particular who diet frequently are more likely to:

★ binge eat

★ purge food (vomit)

★ have poor health

★ become depressed.

Remember – women are meant to have curves (but men aren't meant to have breasts!).

Body image in children

Adopting a healthy lifestyle is the best way to manage your weight and model healthy behaviours for your children. Use the following to encourage positive beliefs about body image at home:

★ Avoid calling foods 'good' or 'bad' – try 'everyday' foods and 'sometimes' foods.

★ Model eating all foods. For example, when eating 'sometimes' foods, such as chocolate or sweets, show your child that it is OK to eat them slowly and enjoy them without feeling guilty. This is much better than eating them quickly, secretively or all at once.

★ Avoid using food as a punishment or overusing it as a reward.

★ Don't tell your child to lose weight – encourage the whole family to adopt healthy eating patterns and regular physical activity.

★ Tell your children that you love them unconditionally – and tell them that a lot.

★ Avoid using extreme weight-loss practices yourself.

★ Make time to eat as a family frequently and make meal times enjoyable and stress free. Don't make eating habits a big issue.

★ Make sure there are plenty of nutritious foods in the house and limit access to less nutritious foods.

★ Encourage your children to listen to signals from their body – when they're hungry and when they've had enough.

- ★ You may wish to serve food in the centre of the table so each person can serve their own size portions according to their appetite.
- ★ Don't make your children eat everything on their plate (a throw back to rationing), but do encourage them to at least taste some of the food.
- ★ Raise children so they associate 'treat' with special kinds of fruit, or something else nutritious, instead of sweets.

If you need support, seek professional advice from someone who specialises in childhood weight issues.

BRILL BIT

Write a list of 10 things you like about your body. Keep it in a safe place and when you don't like what you see in the mirror look at the list instead.

Sleep and meditation

Which best describes you?

'Not getting enough sleep is a surefire way to make me feel lousy. It's not that I need much, 14–15 hours a night and a couple of naps during the day is all I ask, but I'm just not getting my quota.'

Or:

'I'm so lucky: four or five hours a night and I've got all the energy I need! Sleep? I can take it or leave it!'

My guess is you're closer to the first than the second and that's why you're reading this section.

Tips to help you sleep

If you get broken sleep or you find it hard to 'drop off' in the first place then here are a few tips to help you:

★ Aim to get to bed on the right side of 11.00 (that's pm!). This is much more restorative to your adrenal glands than sleep that begins later at night (even if you sleep late the next morning).

★ Prioritise sleep. You will achieve much more with your day if you have had a good six to eight hours' sleep.

★ It is important to feel physically tired before going to bed – this is where exercise is vital.

★ Avoid caffeine or large amounts of fluid for a few hours before going to bed – uninterrupted sleep is ideal.

★ If you can't get six to eight hours, at least make sure the time you spend in the bedroom is productive and relaxing, i.e. don't watch television or do work.

★ A relaxing salt bath is a wonderful way to help your body to relax before you go to bed. The salts continue to work overnight too.

Did you know 85% of all healing occurs when you are in deep sleep?

Meditation

Meditation or other methods of deep relaxation can improve your health dramatically. Relaxation of all kinds decreases cortisol and epinephrine levels in the blood and helps to balance your biochemistry. In simple terms that means it lowers blood pressure and prevents depression.

In most Western cultures we aren't taught how to meditate properly, if at all. Instead we are told to stop daydreaming and to pay attention.

Six steps to excellent meditation

1 Exercise first to create energy and good circulation.

2 Sit with a comfortable, balanced posture. Your spine should be straight, muscles relaxed, chin in slightly. If in a chair, distribute your weight equally so your hips are balanced.

3 Shift attention to your breath. Pay attention to in- and outflow. Mentally scan your body as you become relaxed, still and fully present.

4 Choose the meditation you will practise. Prepare to take on the posture, movement, breathing pattern and/or sounds you will use.

5 As you begin, let your flow of thoughts pass by and move to the background. Any thought that 'grabs' you, just watch it float away or focus and replace it.

6 Gradually increase the length of time you meditate – don't expect to become 'enlightened' during your first session.

BRILL BIT

If you find it difficult to drift off to sleep, when you go to bed visualise each part of your body from your scalp to your toes relaxing and say in your mind 'I'm falling into a deep relaxing sleep' five times for each body part. You'll drift off much faster and have a deeper, better quality sleep.

PART TWO
YOUR FAMILY

PART TWO
VALUATION

5

THE FAMILY
WHEEL

The best way to look at, and improve, your family life is to break it down into the 'who's who', as there are often different issues with mums, dads, brothers and sisters, grandparents and children. That's why there are spokes on this wheel for seven different types of family relationships. Of course, you may not have all seven and, in those instances, just miss out that section and plot your wheel in such a way as links the nearest two points either side.

So here's the Family Wheel. First you're going to rate each relationship, as it is now, using the guidance given below. Give yourself honest marks out of 10 (high marks being good, low marks being bad/poor).

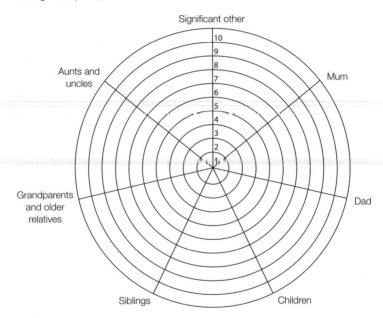

Your significant other

Have you got one? A husband, wife, life partner or lover? Do they rock your world? Or do they wreck your world? Do they make you feel like the most special person in the world or do they make you feel you are last on their list? Is the magic still there? If so, you get a high mark.

On the other end of the scale, it could be that you have lost the initial spark, the relationship is destructive in some way or you're not quite sure where this relationship is going. It could also be that your current relationship with your significant other is somehow limiting your own development or that maybe you've become too dependent and needy. Give yourself a mark out of 10 on the 'Significant other' spoke of your wheel.

Your Mum

So how is your relationship with the person who brought you into this world? Are you very close – best friends even – or have you found yourself growing apart over the years? Do you see your mother as often as you should or are you often too 'busy'? Giving yourself a mark out of 10 for your relationship with your Mum is a tough one, but take a good hard look at your relationship with her and give yourself as truthful a mark as you can.

Your Dad

If you thought marking your relationship with your Mum was hard, marking your relationship with your Dad is even harder. Dads are a funny bunch; I should know as I am one! Do you have a strong loving relationship with your father or have you always found relating to him a little tricky? Perhaps you haven't seen him in a long time or maybe he's your rock. Give yourself a mark out of 10 for your relationship with your Dad.

Your children

Having children is one of the incredible experiences of your life – if not *the* most. If you have them you'll know it is complex, frustrating, rewarding and gratifying and that can all occur before breakfast!

Your job is to measure your relationship with your child or children, as it is now. If you have more than one child, you can add extra spokes and mark the relationship with each of your children.

Do you have incredible kids who make you proud, who do as they are asked, who wouldn't look too out of place in *The Waltons*? Or are they driving you up the wall right now? Is it fabulous or frustrating; does it change each day? Give yourself an honest mark about how you feel your relationship is with your kids.

Your siblings

Brothers? Sisters? One of each, older or younger? When we are growing up they are some of the most important people in our lives, but when we get older and more independent is that still the case?

If you haven't heard from your brother or sister in months and you're not really bothered because you think they are a pain in the neck, then that could be marked high or low. I'll let you decide. What does matter is whether it worries and concerns you – is there something deeper beneath this distance? Or you could be lucky and be thinking, 'My relationship with my brother/sister(s) is amazing, I get high marks here'. Then, well done, give them a call and tell them it's just how you want it to be.

Your grandparents and older relatives

If you have grandparents, lucky you. Mine are just memories now and I miss them. So, if you have a grandparent or grandparents, how do you rate your relationship with them? Have you worked hard to develop a close and loving relationship over the years? Do you see them regularly and do you take care of them? Or is it a chore to go and see them? You have so little in common that you simply do your duty and show your face or call now and then. Give yourself a mark and if you have any other older relatives give yourself a mark for your relationship with them too.

Your aunts and uncles

So how is that aunt/uncle to nephew/niece relationship? It's often the case that we see a lot of our aunts and uncles when we are young, but as we get older we drift apart. Do you know when their birthdays are and do you send them cards? When was the last time you just called in? If you feel comfortable with the time and energy you place in that relationship, then give yourself a nice high mark; if not, you know what to do.

Adding it all up

Now join up the scores to see how your Family Wheel is looking. Once you've done that you could argue that getting a low mark in some areas is OK as you get higher marks in the 'most important areas' of the wheel. I agree, but as you did the exercise, if there was a little tug on your heart as you scored a low mark in an area, then turn to that chapter and see if there is a message there for you.

6

YOUR SIGNIFICANT OTHER

aving an intimate relationship with someone whom you love so much you could pop is just about as good as it gets. It's most people's goal, yet few achieve it and even fewer maintain it.

I've been married twice. Not unusual these days, but I've been married twice to the same person. I don't know if she just couldn't live without me (joke), but I know I couldn't imagine life without her (serious). So, why did we split up you may be asking? I'll be honest with you – it wasn't helped by the fact I'd stopped doing my Wheel of Life.

Once I discovered this brilliant tool in 1991 I completed it every month for eight years. Then I started to teach personal development and I became so focused on my business I forgot to do my own Wheel of Life. If I had, I might have spotted much earlier that my Family Wheel was suffering and, in particular, my relationship with my wife.

I live with my wife and work with her. We do everything together – it's brilliant. The reason it works is because we work at it every single day. When you've lost something special and then get a second chance you don't want to lose it again. But isn't it ironic that this amazing and special relationship can be taken for granted?

Taking your relationship for granted is the thin end of the wedge and if you don't correct it soon then you may have a challenge on your hands.

Repairing your relationship

If you've realised that your relationship isn't what it should be, and you want to do something about it, you need to know that this may not be an easy journey. You really have to ask yourself whether you are willing to put the effort in to get things back on track – half-hearted efforts can often do more damage than good.

However, if you do decide you want to make the relationship work brilliantly again, and you are prepared to really give it your all, then take heart – it may seem like an impossible task at first, but often simple changes can have a profound effect.

Here are 10 things you can do right now to set you off in the right direction:

1   Start dating each other again. Do you remember how much effort you put into your relationship when it was new and exciting? Go on some dates and make the same effort as you did first time around.

2   Say sorry. Even if it's not your fault.

3   Be there. Many relationships fail because people get absorbed in their own world – be there for your partner.

4   Write love notes. They don't have to be soppy sonnets; just say how much you appreciate what your partner does for you.

5   Cook a meal together. Admittedly for some people that could be the start of the divorce but, for most, cooking together is a great way to get closer.

6   Be interested in them. Ask your partner questions and be fascinated by the answers.

7   Give genuine compliments. Tell them what you like, not what's wrong.

8   Cut down on or stop watching TV. Especially in the bedroom (you can work that one out).

9   Remember what was right. By going to the best bits of your past you can create better bits for your future.

10   Do the Wheel of Life together.

Adopt the right approach

One of the reasons why many relationships fail is because the main purpose of the relationship is forgotten or the intimacy of the relationship is moved to one side.

When I was separated from my wife, I travelled to Australia to see Tony Robbins present his 'Date with Destiny' seminar. At exactly 11 pm on 10 April 2002, I saw him explain the three levels of relationships and at that moment made a decision that I was only going to be satisfied with a Level 3 relationship – I know it was exactly then, because I wrote it down and I keep that piece of paper close by at all times.

The three levels of a relationship are:

★ *Level 1*: What can I get out of this relationship?

★ *Level 2*: I'll do this for you but I expect you to do that for me.

★ *Level 3*: Your needs are my needs.

When I first heard those words I realised that in the past I had managed on a Level 2 relationship and when the marriage failed I had taken the relationship to Level 1.

If you focus on moving towards Level 3, you'll feel differently about your relationship – you'll come from a place of complete care for the other person first. If your partner is doing the same a Level 3 relationship is blissful. It's rare that anyone can be like this all the time in every situation, but it is a wonderful goal and when you have this intention at heart you'll find yourself scoring top marks in no time.

And the best time to start is right now. Tell your partner how much you love them, write that note, make an effort and who knows, your spark could be reignited, your flame fanned and your relationship taken to another level.

BRILL BIT

Always treat your partner the way you'd like, no, actually *love*, to be treated. Even if you don't feel they are behaving very well towards you. That's the real test.

7

YOUR MUM

If you've recognised that your relationship with your Mum needs some extra attention, then good for you. The advice that follows is split it into three parts. One for those who scored under 4, one for those who scored from 4 to 7 and one for those who are an 8 plus.

Under 4

If you scored under 4, you've probably got a fairly deep-rooted issue to deal with. Your priority then is not to try to score 10, but just to aim to get a few more points and edge things gently in the right direction.

You are who you are today because of how you interpret the world around you. What may seem like a difficult relationship with your mother to you may seem completely normal to someone else. That's why there is no set way to improve this relationship, but there are some things you can do that will have an immediate effect.

Start talking

If you have some resentment towards your mother (or vice versa), it's worthwhile taking the time to explain how you are feeling. Most importantly, *DON'T* look for an explanation, an apology or solution, just share how you feel. It's a powerful first step.

Remember the good times

If you choose to dwell on the bad times your focus will ultimately end up on the bad times. Remember, you get what you focus on. Choose to remember the good – there will be some.

Use an intermediary

Often an aunt/uncle or family friend can be of help if you are having challenges communicating directly.

Or it may be that you don't want to have a relationship with your mother. My wife has chosen that road and she's very happy. She always saw her grandmother as the person she would call

Mum after her natural mother chose not to raise her. She's very comfortable about this and would never let it affect her Family Wheel of Life.

4 to 7

My guess is at least you're speaking. Perhaps you gave yourself this mark because you don't seem as close to your mother as you could be or you haven't seen her as often as you'd like.

Remember, it is a mother's job to worry unnecessarily and be overly concerned with the smallest of things. The intention behind any apparent interfering is very likely to be concern on Mum's part; she's not really meddling, she's just showing how worried she is. It's just that that her 'concern' is driving you nuts!

Here are four tips for you to help you get on better with your mother in these kind of situations:

1 Give her some significance. Often when mothers are seen to be intrusive it's because they no longer seem to be relied on. By giving your mother (or mother-in-law) some significance you can often help her to cut down on the amount of 'interfering' she does.

2 Give them a role. Mothers love worry, so give her something important to worry about or take responsibility for.

3 Call them for no other reason than to say: 'I just called for a chat.' Then ask her lots of questions.

4 Tell her you love her. Mums never tire of hearing it and if you haven't said it for a while then now is a good time to do it.

8 plus

So, your relationship is pretty good but you want it to be brilliant. Yes? OK, here's what you can do. Simple ways to get bonus marks with Mum.

★ Take your Mum shopping and don't be in a hurry. Or do anything she enjoys without being in a hurry. Mums often feel their children don't have the time for them and are rushed around.

★ Don't wait for Mother's Day. Have something special delivered. Find something other than flowers – everyone does flowers.

★ Arrange a weekend away. It may be a quick trip for you but mums will love the build-up, adore the time and delight in the memories.

★ Find an old family video film (or 'cine') and have it put on to DVD, then arrange a special showing. You'll be amazed at how much you have all grown up.

BRILL BIT

Just think what your mother did so you could be here. No matter at what level your relationship stands at the moment, it's worth remembering what she did for you so you can be here, reading this right now.

8

YOUR DAD

It's a father's role to embarrass his children at every available opportunity. I said I would never do it but suddenly found I was getting the 'Dad, you are sooo embarrassing!' line. I don't know how it happened but what I did learn is that there is no such thing as being a cool Dad. So, with that in mind, and writing as a Dad, I've got a few thoughts on this one.

If you've hit rock bottom …

Let's start with the very low marks. If you've hit rock bottom with this one you either have seriously strong negative feelings towards your father, you don't see him or both.

So, what if you just don't see him? The first question is: 'Do you want to do something about it?' You may be very happy not having a father in your life. But if you do then step one is a tough one. How do you make contact? I had a friend in this situation once, so I suggested she write a letter. Good idea but after four weeks she still hadn't written anything and the reason? 'I don't know how to start.'

So, here's an idea for an opening paragraph:

Dear Dad

It's not easy for me to write this letter and I am guessing it's not easy for you to read it. But I had to write because I believe you and I have a few things we need to sort out to make both of our lives happier.

And here are a few thoughts on what should come next:

★ a positive paragraph about where you are now
★ a few lines about what was good about your relationship
★ a very clear section on what you want – be specific
★ a final thought.

If the relationship is strained

If you are doing OK, but not brilliantly, then here are some thoughts for you:

★ Organise a Dads' and lads' or Dads' and daughters' day. This is a day for just the two of you. It should be interesting for you both and as far away from normal life as you can make it. The fact that it isn't like normal life gives you both something in common and if you're out of your comfort zones together then that can help.

★ Don't prejudge how your Dad will react to this suggestion – it could be one of your best days ever.

★ Make a fuss. Dads love having a fuss made of them – they say they don't, but they do.

★ Listen to their ramblings. Dads have a unique ability to be able to ramble on and on. Their kids often feel the urge to finish sentences for them. Bite your tongue, as this is a surefire way to make Dads feel less than special.

If you want it to be brilliant

So, your relationship with Dad is really good but you want it to be brilliant!

Here are nine ways to get bonus marks:

1 Take him to the races, the airshow or anywhere else you know he'd enjoy himself.

2 Tell him you love him.

3 Teach him a skill.

4 Be extra patient.

5 Ask him to come round to your house.

6 Do one of his jobs – without being asked.

7 Ask him to help you with something practical.

8 Play a sport together.

9 Ask him to teach you to do something he's good at.

BRILL BIT

Send your Dad a card when it's not Father's Day, his birthday or Christmas.

9

YOUR CHILDREN

In order for me to fulfil my goal of being a brilliant Dad, I aim to be brilliant with my kids – but they have to think I'm brilliant too. Easier said than done, especially when they may not agree with what you're teaching, sharing or discussing with them.

My wife, Christine, who is the most supportive person in the world, often says, 'It's not our job as parents to be popular.' True, it's not. I see so many parents buying the affection of their kids and letting them get away with so much to avoid conflict or to be seen to be 'cool'. This, in turn, makes the situation worse later and the spiral continues in ever-downward circles. I worry when a parent says their child is their best friend. Kids are pushing boundaries and they want you to let them know where those boundaries are. However, the person who points it out *isn't* going to be popular. It's a paradox and very difficult for best friends to do.

Accept responsibility

So, if you are having a challenging relationship with your child, then who's to blame? Well, that's not a very constructive place to start. A better question may be, 'Whose job is it to improve it?'

Unless your kids have read the previous chapters on mums and dads, it's unlikely to be them. So that leaves you!

I remember once coaching a brilliant company director named Jim. Jim had a son aged 16 who was also called Jim (Jim Jnr). As you would expect, we started the first coaching session by completing a Wheel of Life. He had 10s for career, vision and personal development. However, he had a three for family. 'Why the three for family?' I asked him. 'It's my 16-year-old son', he said, 'He's a little ****!' Clearly a good place to start.

After some discussion, I asked him if he loved his son. His reply was: 'Yes, I love him, I just don't like him right now.' So I gave him the homework of telling his son that he loved him.

WEEK 1: Nothing.

WEEK 2: 'I almost told him' (whatever that meant!)

WEEK 3: He did it! The only thing they did have in common was that they supported the same football team – they were watching football on Sky Sports and their team won. This was Jim's moment. He turned to Jim Jnr, took a deep breath and said: 'Jim, I need to tell you something. I love you, son, I want you to know that, I love you.'

Jim Jnr looked his Dad in the eye and asked, 'What do you want?' before walking out of the room shaking his head.

If it had ended there then that would be tragic; however, Jim went on to tell me how later that night his wife had revealed that she knew he'd 'done it' because Jim Jnr had walked straight into the kitchen and said: 'Dad just told me he loves me.' She asked him, 'How does that make you feel?', to which he replied: 'Good, Mum, pretty good.'

When you aren't getting on well with your child, it's very easy to play the 'I'm not saying sorry first' game, but somebody has to, so why not you...? You're the grown up after all.

Take time to talk

As children grow up it's their job to cause worries for parents, but the joy they bring far outweighs the problems – usually. It's worth making sure you have enough time to talk. Mealtimes are perfect for this. Make a real effort to eat together and try opening conversation with a simple 'Tell me about your day.' Notice it's not 'How was your day?' because that question is almost guaranteed to be answered with one word: 'Fine.'

The real secret here is to have lots of follow-up questions because as children get older their desire to communicate with parents reduces – dramatically.

Here are five follow-up questions:

1 What was the best bit about today?

2 What could have been better?

3 What made you laugh?

4 What problems/worries are your friends facing (the subtle way to find out what's going on in *their* minds)?

5 Tell me one thing you've learned today (especially good with younger children).

How to get your kids to tidy their rooms without even asking them

I once did an event for a college and the only way they could get all the staff together was to hold it on a Saturday. The principal was worried that there would be low attendance so I suggested she put on the flyer as part of the list of what they would learn: 'How to get your kids to tidy their rooms without being asked, nagged, cajoled or threatened.'

Ninety-eight per cent of staff turned up – even those who didn't have kids!

The answer is simple. Tell your children how good they are at tidying their rooms. Find the slightest thing they have done and keep on reaffirming how much tidier their room is. Now here's where you need guts and stickability because the tipping point where they actually start to believe you and start cleaning and tidying can take anything from a few days to weeks. YOU HAVE TO STICK WITH IT.

It does work – but you have to believe.

> **BRILL BIT**
>
> If you travel away from home and you are going to be away for more than one night, write to your children. Kids love getting stuff in the post.
>
> Giving children unconditional love when they are babies is easy. But as they grow up they need it even more.

10

YOUR SIBLINGS

Having a brother or sister can be great when you're growing up – for starters there's always somebody around to play with. But when we grow up, we've got to take responsibility and make an effort in the relationship. Otherwise, before you know it, you're meeting at family events a couple of times a year, saying 'we must catch up'.

In my experience, most people have a low mark for their relationships with siblings for one of three reasons:

1 They fell out due to a family issue (usually parents).

2 They don't see each other as they have little in common.

3 Money – something happened financially and they fell out.

How things go wrong

David was very close to his sister Lisa as they grew up. When he started working and 'paying board' she went to college, then on to university. This was followed by a gap year which turned into five.

During this time David worked hard. Shortly after buying a new house, their mother had a stroke and moved in with him, his wife and his eight-month-old daughter. After nine months of care rehabilitation she moved back to her home, but David visited her every day. David cared for his Mum for two years before she died; he arranged the funeral and took care of pretty much everything. When Lisa arrived 'home' for the funeral there was a different feeling between David and his sister. And three weeks later it was about to get a lot worse.

In her will, their Mum left half of her estate to David and half to Lisa. Admittedly David wasn't happy but his wife was furious: 'How could she leave her the same as you? You cared for her, you did everything, it's not fair.' And just at a time when a brother and sister should support each other they were being pushed further apart.

I would love to say the story you have read is a rare occurrence but a friend of mine who is a solicitor tells me it isn't. If you have a situation like that or similar, here's what you can do.

★ *Understand* – spend some time thinking about your parents' motives for doing whatever they have done. Put yourself in their shoes.

* *Communicate* – share how you feel but don't judge; it may be that your sibling feels as uncomfortable as you do.

* *Remember why* you did what you did. I'm sure David didn't do all he did for his Mum because he thought he'd get more of the inheritance.

Focus on what's important

Brothers and sisters often grow apart. Whether geography or beliefs, it's a shame when this happens. I've heard people say: 'I haven't seen my brother in years.' My father went through a period where he didn't see his brother for years. Well, they did see each other, they were living in the same town, but they didn't speak or spend time together. This has changed and now their relationship is brilliant.

So, what happened? I think they went back to the core of their relationship; they focused on what they had in common and built on these foundations. My Uncle Harry has a fantastic allotment; my Dad doesn't, so he started a mini-allotment at the side of his house and asked Harry for help. They talk passionately about grandchildren and use each other's skills to help with home improvements.

By focusing on what's right, they have become very close.

BRILL BIT

It might not be a good idea to keep on play fighting into adulthood. However, do keep the fun and the practical jokes. Honestly, it is worth standing motionless in a cupboard for almost an hour just so you can leap out and scare the living daylights out of your brother. Isn't it, Andrew?

11

YOUR GRANDPARENTS AND OLDER RELATIVES

When I was a youth worker I spent a week working with an amazing friend of mine, Rev. Barrie Lees, in his parish of Falmouth. It was going to be a week working in schools, with the youth club and for the local Boys' Brigade. I'd just started my career and enthusiastically thought young people were the answer to everything!

When Barrie suggested we visit an old folks' home my non-verbal response must have spoken volumes; he looked me in the eye and said: 'Old people are important too.' He was, as always, right and surprisingly enough I plan on being an old person one day too!

I know they drive you nuts, frustrate the life out of you, do things at a third of the speed and think your taste in music is terrible, but how well do you know them?

Here's a little test for you to see how much you know about your grandparents:

★ When are their birthdays?

★ How old are they?

★ What concerns them?

★ What was their first job?

★ What makes them laugh?

Five out of five? Well done! Anything less and you have a few conversation starters for the next time you see them.

How to build the relationship

How do you build a relationship with someone who'll be at least two generations apart from you?

Well, if you have read the other chapters in this section then you'll have probably picked up on a few common themes about staying in touch, showing interest and being proactive. They are all very important, but here's a magic tool you can use with older people and they love it. It's called 'the family reunion'.

My cousin Helen decided to have one of these a couple of years ago for no reason other than she didn't want to see her aunts, uncles, cousins and extended family only at weddings and funerals.

Are you up for it? Now here's the trick: once they've been invited, give everyone who is coming a responsibility. There's something quite special about having a 'do', inviting everyone and giving them a job. Also, remember to make your grandparents the guests of honour. Finally, ask people to bring loads of old photos or videos and to create three questions for a family quiz.

It does take a bit of effort and if asked they would probably say they aren't worth the fuss. Grandparents often feel left out; the world is changing rapidly around them and one of the only constants is their family, so make it brilliant.

BRILL BIT

Here's a lovely idea. Why not record an older relative or grandparent telling stories of their life? It's easy to do and for the investment of some basic recording equipment you can capture some brilliant stories and have a permanent reminder of them.

YOUR AUNTS AND UNCLES

My Aunty Ethel is brilliant. She always remembers birthdays, phones my Mum when she sees me in the newspapers, calls the kids if they have achieved something, buys brilliant presents for Christmas and birthdays and is the perfect hostess if you visit.

I wonder what she would say about her nephew, Michael. Probably that I never remember her birthday, hardly ever call, I am usually too busy to visit and in many ways could be a lot better. But that's the beauty of an Aunty Ethel; she's so forgiving.

Losing the connection

When we are younger these relatives are quite special; because they are 'one step removed' from close family they are an easier group to get on with. As an uncle myself I appreciate my relationship with my nephew and niece as being based on all the fun but with none of the responsibility. Nice.

As we get older, our relationship with our aunts and uncles tends to be much more distant and, for many of us, non-existent. This is a great shame as it is likely there's no great underlying cause – it's simply a case of keeping the connection going

The family tree

As with all family relationships, you've got to think about staying in touch, showing an interest and being proactive.

All of these apply with the aunts' and uncles' area too but there is another magic tool you can use with them as well. It's called the family tree. Have you ever thought about your genealogy? Once you get past great grandparents there tends to be a breakdown in the family records, but now, with the use of technology and the accessibility of records, it's never been easier to study your earlier generations. I bet if you were to go back just five generations you'd find some amazing information that could be shared.

Or finally, why not ask them for their knowledge to help you get started with the project?

Do all of this and you'll be giving yourself much higher marks in the future.

Call in and visit your aunties and uncles completely unannounced. Take them flowers and cakes and tell them what they mean to you.

PART THREE
YOUR MONEY

13

THE MONEY
WHEEL

If I were to pick one area of life that most people have a challenge with, this is it. Money troubles are very common, however, you'll see it's not about how much or little you have.

So take a few minutes to complete your Money Wheel, then you can focus on the areas where you have the lowest marks. It's never as bad as you think when you break it down.

Give yourself a score out of 10 on each topic, using the prompts below to help you decide where you are on the scale.

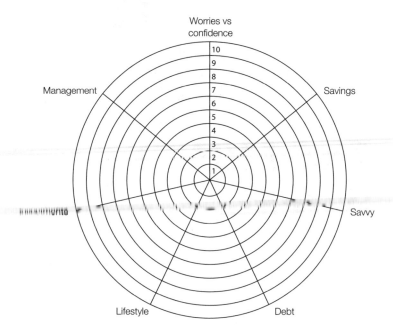

Worries vs confidence

We're starting with a score for your general feelings about money. Specific areas, such as credit cards or your salary, will be covered later. Here we're looking for your underlying gut feel, your attitude, how you generally 'feel' about finances. So, if you feel super confident, it's a high mark; if you worry about money all the time, it's low. You may be somewhere in between but follow your gut on this one and give yourself a mark.

Savings

Do you have any? Some people spend everything they earn, others always save no matter what they earn – it's a mindset. If you think 'If I earned more then I would start to save' then I'm afraid it's a lower mark and, of course, if you have savings well in place then it's high.

Savvy

Savvy here means the financial know-how. You know, that knowledge that some people have and others envy. Are you one of those people who have a flair for spotting good deals and actually enjoy 'playing' with money? Or are you bewildered by the world of finance and unsure if you are getting the best deals or advice?

Debt

You may be surprised to learn that you are not going to mark yourself here on your level of debt. Some of the best deals in the world have been funded using 'OPM' (other people's money). It's about your control and management of debt.

When those ads appear on TV claiming that 'because of a little known piece of government legislation you can have your debts written off', do you think 'Wow, should I give them a call'? Low marks if this is you!

If, however, you feel happy about your level of debt and how it helps you to live your lifestyle and leverage your money without worry, then you get a high mark.

Debt is subjective. Some people believe you should have no debt, others see it as an enabler. That's why you are going to HONESTLY score yourself for how you *feel* about debt and how you handle that feeling now.

Lifestyle

Do you make the most of cash-saving opportunities or does your lifestyle cost you a fortune? I'm not talking about being a Scrooge for scrimping or an Elton John for a lavish lifestyle; just simply, is your lifestyle beyond or within your income?

If you live well within it's a high mark. If you spend more than you earn it's a very low mark. And if you've never considered it then that's a low mark, too!

Investments

Do you know how to invest? Do you know the difference between a good and a bad investment? Do you know the difference between cash savings and investments? Have I confused you already?

If you have good investments that are working well for you then you'll get high marks here; no investments and you get low marks, and for making some poor investments you can have midway marks – at least you're trying!

Management

If you have good money management skills you'll know exactly how much you have in your bank account right now. You'll know how much you owe, when it's due and have a clear plan as to when you are going to pay it.

If you have poor financial management then you'll feel like you are in the dark when it comes to your finances – you'll probably have standard excuses like: 'I'm just not very good at managing my money.' At the end of the day you are doing this exercise for you and you alone, so give yourself an honest mark.

So, that's it, your Money Wheel is complete. Join up the marks and notice the areas where you could do with some money magic. Some of the advice I'm about to give will be a challenge but if you take action it will also be one of the most rewarding things you will ever do.

It's time to turn to the chapters where you have a lower mark and take action where action is most needed.

14

WORRIES VS CONFIDENCE

So, how do you turn money worries into money confidence? The obvious answer would be 'earn more money'. However, I've done this exercise with people who have made over £5 million in a year and they still worry about money. I've also done this exercise with people who earn less than £5000 a year and their money confidence is sky high.

I once did a Wheel of Life with a Premiership Footballer, and was astounded when he gave himself a very low mark for money. He was earning more money in a week than most people did in a year and still he worried. He worried that it might stop. He worried about funding his lifestyle. He worried that lots of people wanted a bit (or a lot) of his money. He worried that he wouldn't be able to help his family the way he wanted to. And he worried whether or not his financial advisors were giving him the best financial advice. All in all, he worried way too much about money.

You may be reading this and thinking 'I wish I had his money worries' and I can't blame you, but the fact is he would have worried about money if he earned £5 or £5 million.

At the other end of the scale is Alfie, who lives in Ibiza. He hangs out on the beach and busks during the summer. You couldn't meet a person who has fewer money worries. It may be because he has no money to worry about, but, hey, that's Alfie's choice. And it is his choice, because at one point in his life Alfie was an insurance broker earning a six-figure income and killing himself with worry.

How much do you worry?

Here's the thing – money is just a form of energy, it flows in and it flows out. Some people have large flows of money, with huge incomes and huge outgoings to match – but they are completely relaxed about it. Others have large incomes and small outgoings yet still they worry.

Here are five questions to ask yourself:

1 If I lost all my money tomorrow what would I do?

2 How do I feel about paying tax?

3 What did my parents teach me about money?

4 How much is too much?

5 What creates my money worries for me?

By answering these five simple questions about money you'll find out a lot about yourself. If you have a life partner, it will be fascinating to answer those questions together too.

Alleviate your money worries

So, if money is causing stresses and worries here are five things you can do to alleviate some of the worries:

1 Read every chapter in this section, do the exercises and act on the advice.

2 Find someone who appears to have little in the way of either money or worries and ask them their secrets.

3 Talk about money. We are taught not to talk about money. I've found that the people who are happy to talk about money (not brag) are often the most relaxed people who have the best tips.

4 Help someone (not necessarily financially) who is less fortunate than you. It's interesting how your own money worries seem to shrink when you find out about other people's needs.

5 Create an affirmation that asserts your confidence with money. It may sound like you're faking it at first but you'll quickly start to believe it, then do it.

Worrying unnecessarily about money creates negative spirals that quickly drag you down. It's challenging to break these beliefs when you are at rock bottom but anyone can, and if that's you I can confidently tell you that with the knowledge you will acquire in the next few pages you will.

BRILL BIT

The single biggest challenge with 'money worries' is not facing up to the fact that you have them. Recognise you have a challenge then use the energy you are putting into worrying to start making a positive impact on the problem.

15

SAVING

We all know we should save, but where's the incentive? Is it on your 'too difficult' list? What if I was to persuade you that saving can be easier than you think? The challenge is we live in a world where you aren't encouraged to save. Quite the opposite; you're more likely to be encouraged to get credit and 'have it now and pay for it later' than to save. There are times when credit (i.e. borrowing money) is a reasonable option – after all, how many people do you know who saved up for their house before they bought it? Very few people save for a car or a holiday these days. So why bother saving at all? Once again it's down to mindset. You know deep down you should save. We hear expressions about putting something away for a rainy day and appreciate the concept but not the action. Mind you, where I live it rains every other day!

Small steps reap great rewards

I've been through three phases in my life when it comes to saving. When I was very young my parents encouraged me to save; even if it was just a little bit of money after a birthday or Christmas going into my building society account. I was never allowed to get my hands on the account book. When I started work aged 16 in 1983, I was given the book and was amazed to see that I had saved £1280 in the first 16 years of my life!

The chances are high that you are reading this and thinking: 'What's the big deal, £1280 isn't a lot of money.' But I managed to buy a car before my 17th birthday and learnt to drive in my own motor. I can't tell you how good it felt to drive my own car in my driving test! By the time I was 22, I had spent all the money and some. I'd bought my first house and I would now spend everything I earned (and more). In the back of my mind I knew one day I could start saving again. The point was I didn't. I didn't have the discipline and without the discipline I would never save.

I was lucky though; two years later I married 'a saver' and she helped me to get back into the habit and opened some 'savings accounts'. Even though we were only just married and needed money for all sorts of things we still saved. We saved for holidays, we saved for cars, we saved for home improvements and after a few short years we realised an interesting thing. Even though we knew people who had similar incomes to ourselves, who often got things 'faster', we were now very comfortable. I was going to write 'very lucky' there but the more I look at how we set out to create our lifestyle, the decisions we made and the effort it took, I realise less and less is down to luck.

Create the saving mindset

Becoming a saver is a long-term plan. It's not just about what you are saving for, it's about the feeling of having saved – it's amazing. And once you do it a couple of times it becomes a mindset. Don't think you have to earn more to be able to keep and save more money.

Here are 20 ideas to help you save:

1   Open a savings account and set up a direct debit to pay a monthly amount straight into it.

2   Set some savings goals and write them down.

3   Give up something you do 'just because you always have' and save that money.

4   Make saving fun by creating a reward system for yourself (not cash!).

5   Save all your loose change each day and put it in your savings account once a week.

6   Wait 48 hours before you buy something expensive or outside your normal weekly shopping; if you have decided you don't really need it, save the money you would have spent.

7   Be super frugal! Turn off the lights, repair rather than rebuy, become tight for 90 days and put away every penny saved. By turning off your lights when they aren't being used and turning your thermostat down by just a degree you'll save over £100 a year.

8   Save a windfall – you weren't expecting it, so pop it away.

9   Use vouchers and coupons – £10 a week is £520 a year in your savings account.

10 Take your lunch to work. It costs 50p and saves a minimum of £2 a day. That's another £500 a year.

11 Quit a bad habit you pay for – see the Health Wheel for ideas.

12 Shop around; when you get a deal bank the difference into your savings account.

13 Sell a bunch of stuff on eBay or at a car boot sale; people will actually buy stuff you don't want or need!

14 Use your library. But still buy my books – as they are an investment!

15 Stop buying lottery tickets – it *won't* be you!

16 Learn to cook and stop buying 'ready meals'. It's healthier and you save squillions.

17 Drive sensibly. If your car has an MPG meter make it a challenge to be more economical than the day before rather than faster.

18 Only carry a £1 coin with you. Scary but it's amazing what you don't or can't buy.

19 Have friends round for a 'bring a bottle' rather than going out. Before they leave, ask whose turn it will be next.

20 Avoid paying for car parking. Set off earlier, park out of town and walk in. Obviously be safe but think of the health benefits, too.

All these ideas will help you get started and the little bits do add up. But let me give you this final challenge. What if you saved a lot? What if you decided to save 20, 30 or even 50% of your income? It would be a challenge but the bigger the effort the bigger the reward.

BRILL BIT

If you have debts, start to save before you have paid all your debt off. This may seem crazy and financially you will pay more but it will get you into a saving mindset, which is so important.

16

SAVVY

All too often, the mere mention of 'finances' and people get a look of panic or glaze over. But it really doesn't need to be that way. Being financially savvy needn't necessarily mean you have to struggle desperately to understand everything (in a world that is incomprehensible to you) or immerse yourself in something that you find interminably dull. This is just about having a grasp of the basic *principles* and knowing what you can do to stay ahead of the game.

Test your 'savviness'

What is APR and what does it really mean?

Well, if you said it's annual percentage rate, you're right but do you know what that really *means*? If you said it's the actual cost of the loan, including interest, fees and charges, you are savvy. And you'll know it's important to know that, so when one loan looks cheaper than another you won't get overexcited, sign up and suddenly have a bunch of additional costs coming your way.

'Store card' vs 'credit card' – which is better for you?

Well, most store cards have a more expensive APR than credit cards and many are double what you'd pay if you used a credit card. But you may believe you can definitely pay off the store card immediately. In this case, it may be beneficial to take a store card that offers a promotional discount and use this benefit. The fact is, though, the stores know 90% of people who intend to pay off the debt straight away don't.

Which is the better deal: £1000 cash now or £1 now which doubles every day for 14 days?

Well, if you took the £1000 now you'd be better off today than you would with the 14-day deal but worse off at the end of the fortnight. What a difference a day makes and what a difference a year makes too, especially on repayments! The financially savvy know this and they don't get caught up in the idea that a lower monthly repayment looks sexy because they spread the term over a couple of extra years. They look at the whole picture and make informed decisions on the whole amount to be repaid.

Your five-point guide to becoming financially savvy

1 Don't be afraid to ask what may seem like a dumb question when people are asking you to invest in a financial product, use a payment scheme or take a card they are selling to you. Don't buy until you are happy.

2 Read the financial pages on websites and in newspapers, and read books. There's a mass of information. Interestingly, some of it conflicts, but by reading it you'll know what feels right for you and quickly form your own opinion.

3 Ask yourself 'what if' questions. What if I saved for this? What if I didn't buy it at all? What if I shopped around, where would I start? What if I got someone to invest in this with me?

4 Hang out with people who are financially savvy. You become like the people you spend most of your time with. Have some really good questions up your sleeve when you meet with them.

5 Start telling yourself you are financially savvy. Most people are comfortable with telling themselves they are 'thick' when it comes to money. Guess what? If that's what you keep telling yourself then that's what you'll become.

Becoming financially savvy isn't difficult, but the benefits are vast. You'll get better deals, you'll be more effective with your financial management and you'll build your cash confidence.

BRILL BIT

As American financial expert Suze Orman says, 'It's better to do nothing with your money than something you don't understand.' Make it your mission to understand, at least the headline principles!

DEBT

It's the biggest industry in the world, so no wonder you're part of it. And it's no wonder it's so big. There's nothing to manufacture save the odd bit of plastic, no distribution costs and it lasts and lasts.

Here's my take on it ...

Debt is great when you're using it in the right way. Controlled debt to expand a business, buy a house, go on a dream holiday, improve your home, etc., is liberating.

Fred Tilney, whom I acknowledge as the person who invented '12 months' interest-free credit', allowed people of the small town of Leadgate, in the north-east of England, to own a hi-fi or a new television when they could previously only have dreamed of it.

Sir Peter Vardy made it possible for people from small mining villages to buy themselves a new car. As he said: 'They deserved to drive a new car and I helped them to find a way.'

The darker side of debt

However, there's another side to credit and, unfortunately, it has become an epidemic in some parts of our society. And the solution to getting out of debt is often presented as 'take more (or a different kind of) debt'.

If you do an internet search on 'how to get out of debt', you will be inundated by dozens of 'offers' to see if you qualify for 'debt consolidation', 'a new loan' or 'that little known piece of government legislation'; in fact, there are over 100 sponsored links. To put this into context, when you search on 'how to save money' there are half the pages and only five sponsored links.

Clearing debt is a big challenge. It will have a huge impact on what you do and will require a big change of mindset. But once you have put some simple changes in place and are working towards an end goal, you'll be amazed at how good you feel for taking on the challenge.

The five things you must do if you're suffering from debt

1 Get rid of all your cards other than one debit card that you can use at the bank, etc. Don't just push them into a drawer, really get rid of them. Cut them into little pieces and throw them away (divide disposal of them between two litter bins to avoid identity theft).

2 Write a list of all your debts. BE HONEST. Note down the level of interest you are paying each month for each loan or line of credit. It may be that you can benefit from consolidating all of your debts – but shop around and get advice. Consolidating is not always a good idea. The main reason you are in debt is because you spend more than you earn. Consolidation can often lull you into a false sense of security so you continue to spend. Beware: if you consolidate your current debts into your mortgage you are signing up for a long-term deal where your house can be taken if you default.

3 Create a plan to pay off all of your debts other than your mortgage (if you have one) over a sensible period of time. This may be up to 10 years but it will be worth it. Time flies and before you know where you are you'll be able to pay off more than you had planned and the debt will be cleared much more quickly. Use 'snowballing' (see the following Brill bit) as a rapid way to help you to do this.

4 Use the 20 savings ideas in the saving chapter to help you clear more debts and avoid creating new ones.

5 START NOW. This is one area where procrastination will cost you dearly.

BRILL BIT

Snowballing your debt is a clever technique if you have several different liabilities such as credit cards, loans and store cards. It basically means you pay the minimum payments for all your debts other than the one with the highest interest rate. Then you focus the rest of your available repayment money on this, the highest one. Once the one with the

►

highest interest rate is paid off, you focus on the next one and so on until you have cleared your debt. This method can save you thousands and reduce debt payment time significantly.

Now here's a twist championed by a debt management expert called Dave Ramsey. He suggests a similar system but rather than putting your debts in interest rate order you put them in amount order and pay off the *lowest* first, then the next lowest and so on. Although this method will normally mean you pay more interest, you get the fantastic early psychological boost of having paid off some of your debts quickly.

LIFESTYLE

Probably one of the most common reasons people have money problems is because they live a lifestyle that either perfectly matches their income (spend all you earn) or, more commonly, they live a lifestyle that is beyond their means (spend more than you earn).

David Grant CBE, the former Lord Lieutenant of County Durham, whom I knew from my fundraising days, once gave me a brilliant piece of advice about living beyond your means. He said: 'If you can't afford it, face facts – you can't. Don't buy it. If you think you can just about afford it you probably can't so still don't buy it. And if you are certain you can afford it then try and get it in a sale.'

The 'appearance' of wealth

I never really knew what he meant by that until I became involved in a business where image was everything … and I got a taste for expensive cars. I agree expensive is relative but I was sure people would be judging me by the type of car I was driving, so I pushed the boat out and bought a huge Mercedes. I must say for the first few months it was something else – lots of admiring glances and 'life must be good' comments.

Then it needed a service. I remember looking at the servicing bill, thinking: 'I could buy a car for that.' A few admiring glances and comments later my ego was suitably polished and I was smiling again. Well, that was until it needed a new set of tyres. Then when I crashed it one icy night and had to have the wing resprayed, I started to go off my pride and joy. And just when I was feeling down about it, the new model came out and I still had three years left to pay on the old one!

However, it gets worse, because when you have that kind of car people think you are 'minted'. It was always me who was expected to pay for the first round, chip in for this and that, source amazing gifts and be 'the life and soul'. For those of you reading this who spent time with me then, here's a confession – I couldn't afford the lifestyle!

Looking back at those times, I have to laugh – it was all about what other people thought and once I'd created the image I had to stick with it. The point is my real friends didn't care, my wife didn't care and my kids didn't care.

Reality check

So, if you're living a lifestyle that's costing way too much here are a few ideas to help you get back in check:

★ Who are you doing it for? Is it for you or is it for 'them'? If it's for you, ask yourself if it's the authentic you. If it's for them, then it will be a good test of friendships and relationships when the spending stops.

★ Become values driven. There aren't too many people who want to have a value of 'lifestyle beyond my means' but it might be quite good fun to have 'best value' or 'frugality' as one of your principles.

★ Learn to say no (or versions of it): 'Not right now.' 'Can I get back to you?' 'I'll need to check in with someone first.' These are all wimpier (but effective) ways of saying the big NO!

★ Tell your 'friends' you are under investigation. Don't say by whom or about what, but insist you need to keep a low profile and can't be seen spending for a while.

★ Slow down and shop around. A friend of mine bought a Mercedes around six months after me. It was exactly the same model only a different colour. He'd saved thousands by bidding for it at a car auction. As he paid for it the cashier commented: 'Nice car, great price and all because someone was living beyond their means.'

BRILL BIT

When he was 16, my son got a part-time job. He devised a clever little system where, before he spent anything, he would have to calculate how many hours he would need to work to earn that amount of money. Many times he decided it wasn't worth the time and effort before he even had to consider the price.

How much time and effort do you have to put in to earn the cost of the latest 'must have'?

19

INVESTMENT

Most people can save, but few choose to invest for one of these three reasons:

1 Belief they haven't got enough money to invest.

2 Fear of failure.

3 Not knowing how to.

How much is enough?

So, if many people believe they need more money before they can start to invest, how much is enough? £100, £1000, £10,000? Actually, I really do believe you can start to learn how to invest with as little as £200. It's more about getting started than waiting until you have 'enough'. And when you do have enough, you won't want to risk losing it by making the wrong investments because you have no experience.

Fear of failing

Investing can seem very daunting and many fear the risks are too great. Of course, in reality, investment, if approached the right way, needn't be high risk at all. Here's an idea to get you started and to help you overcome that fear.

Imagine you have three barrels that are standing on top of one another. The top barrel is your easy-access barrel, which is used for day-to-day living expenses. Your second barrel is for safe investments. And the third (bottom) barrel is your higher-risk investments.

Your job is to fill the barrels top to bottom. In the top barrel (the one that gives you easy access), you need to have enough money stored in there to pay for three months' worth of expenses. So, if you have a lifestyle which costs £1000 per month you need £3000 in that barrel. It's fair to say if you don't have any current investments then that may seem like a big task and not a very sexy one as you'll be putting the money into a building society or bank account, or perhaps maximising a tax-efficient government incentive to save.

However, once you have filled that barrel any excess will start to pour over into your second barrel. This includes the money you were putting into the first barrel plus the interest the first barrel produces. This barrel should be built to hold the equivalent of 6 to 12 months' salary and invested in safer investments such as blue-chip companies with excellent steady growth records, property and legitimate investment schemes.

Finally, your third barrel will start to fill with the overflow from the success of barrel number two. You can use this to further invest in the areas from barrel two or you can take some higher-risk investment opportunities. This barrel should have enough invested to pay for your current (or desired) lifestyle with the income from the capital. Here's the exciting bit – you get to spend what overflows from barrel three!

It may take you many years to fill all three barrels but the most important thing to do is to make a start. If you don't do it now, you'll kick yourself later.

Not knowing how

That's like saying, 'I don't know how to cook so I'll just starve'. You can find out the basic hows by reading a few books, asking people and bringing it to the forefront of your attention. A word of warning from a very old friend – you don't eat everything you see so don't believe everything you hear!

Invest and invest again

When your investments start to pay, the real key is to reinvest the interest. It will be tempting to take the interest and spend it – you'll say things like: 'Haven't I done well, I deserve it.' It's tough, but every great investor has used the same formula of reinvesting their returns to create their highly-successful investment portfolios. Here's why: two magic words: 'compound' and 'interest'.

Did you know that if you invested £1000 now with an annual return of just 4% you would have £7,106 in 50 years? That may seem like a long time, a low rate, a poor return and nothing to get excited about. But what if you invested an additional £1000 every year? You'd have £165,880 after 50 years. Still not exciting enough? What if you learn to be a brilliant investor? What if you invest £5000 a year every year over 30 years with around a 10% return? Congratulations, you've just made a million! The younger you are the slower you can go; the mistakes you can afford to make can be bigger – and you'll get bigger returns.

If you don't have the knowledge, you can learn it!

Today you can go on investment courses, join clubs and learn online. There are dozens of excellent books available on how to invest and I'm sure you'll find the right thing for you.

> *'It's far better to buy a wonderful company at a fair price than a fair company at a wonderful price.'* (WARREN BUFFETT, THE THIRD RICHEST MAN ON THE PLANET (AND ALL FROM INVESTING))

Ah, and one more thing – your house is *not* an investment. It seems silly with everything you read about property prices, but unless you plan to sell it and use the money then your house is, in fact, a *liability*. That's OK, though, as we all need somewhere to live, just don't fall into the trap of saying: 'My house has gone up in value by £X, aren't I a good investor.'

BRILL BIT

It's a well-documented story that in 1626 Peter Minuit bought Manhattan Island for the equivalent of $24 worth of beads and trinkets. But did you know that if you had invested that money in a treasury-backed government investment programme and the interest was compounded, you would have enough money to buy back Manhattan Island now!

MANAGEMENT

Being in control of your money rather than money having control of you is one of the fundamental principles of having a balanced Money Wheel.

Here are some questions for you. How much money do you have in the bank? How much do you owe? How much income do you need to support your life the way you live it right now? What is your net worth today?

If you know the answers to those questions then you are well on your way to being a brilliant money manager. If, like many, you 'haven't got a clue' then here's what you must do.

Complete a full and frank personal financial audit

Doesn't that sound exciting? If you have a low mark for money management, you're probably panic stricken at the thought or have a heavy heart at the prospect of doing something so incredibly dull.

So, how can I help to give you the motivation to do it? I could say that, if you don't, the chances are your need for financial management and lack of awareness will cost you thousands, give you unnecessary stress then ultimately could even direct you into a downward spiral until you become a bankrupt.

Or I could just say the feeling you get when your finances are in order is right up there with receiving an unexpected tax rebate. Your choice, but it's something that needs to be done.

So, let me take you by the hand and help you through the process.

The bank reconciliation

This is a vitally important place to start and, as most people have a bank account, it's a brilliant way to check your current 'cash' position. This doesn't mean notes and coins in your pocket; it's about keeping a careful eye on your cash flow.

Here's a simple way do it.

Take a start point. This may be your last bank statement. Then over a period of, say, one month record all cheques, standing orders and debit card slips. At the end of the month, take your bank statement and check off your card receipts, cheque stubs, known direct debits and standing orders against your statement.

Then take any uncashed cheques, uncleared debit transactions or amounts you know you have spent but have not yet cleared (not yet appeared on your bank statement) and take them from the total. Then add any money, cheques or amounts that have been deposited into your account since your last statement. The total is your true cash position. Note this is not your net worth – you'll find that out in a minute.

This simple process does several things:

★ It ensures you know the true amount in your account.

★ It helps prevent fraud, double payments and mistakes.

★ It raises your awareness of what you are spending.

★ It gives you peace of mind that you have started to manage your money.

The monthly budget

For one month keep receipts for EVERYTHING you spend. If you can't get a receipt, write it down straight away. Don't think you'll remember to do it at the end of the day; you won't, so write it down as you spend and do it to the penny. You'll use this amount in a moment and it's very important that you don't hide anything.

Fill in the gaps

Income (take any annual figures and divide by 12)

Salary (take-home pay after taxes)	_____
Other monthly incomes	_____
Interest received	_____
Investment income	_____
Any other income	_____
	_____
Total	_____

▶

Expenditure (take major costs annually and divide by 12, i.e. annual holiday £1800/12 = £150)

Mortgage or rent	_____
Utility bills	_____
Car repayments	_____
Car running costs (include servicing)	_____
Debt repayments (credit, store cards, etc.)	_____
Supermarket shopping	_____
Clothing	_____
Entertainment	_____
Eating out	_____
Holiday	_____
Gifts	_____
Home improvements	_____
Other misc. expenditure (be honest)	_____
	_____
Total	_____

Now the moment of truth. Take your expenditure total from your income total and turn the remaining amount into a percentage of your income. How did you do?

★ **25% plus:** Well done! You are managing your money well.

★ **10–25%:** You are OK, but could be heading into the danger zone. This is mainly because it's difficult to think of all your expenditure during an exercise like this. The closer you are to 10% the more of a challenge you have.

★ **0–10%:** The danger zone. This is because you are close to spending everything you earn and you probably aren't aware of what you are buying. Do you find yourself saying things like 'I just don't know where the money goes'?

★ **Less than 0%:** HELP! You must take massive immediate action now. You can't hide your head in the sand any longer. It's time to take drastic steps! Cut your costs and get out of that dangerous cycle. THIS IS A MUST – DO IT NOW!

What am I worth?

Have you ever taken the time to work out what you are worth? Here's a simple formula.

Mine all mine

Market value of primary home   _____
Other properties   _____
Business interests   _____
Cash at hand   _____
Investments (value now)   _____
Belongings*   _____
                                      _____

Total A   _____

*Word of warning: belongings should not be valued on what you paid for them. Take into account depreciation for cars, watches, electronic equipment, etc. or appreciation for art (some jewellery), specialist items, etc.

Liabilities (the total amount left to pay – not monthly charges)
Mortgage   _____
Other debts, cards, etc.   _____
Taxes due   _____
Any other amounts outstanding   _____
                                      _____

Total B   _____

Take **Total B** from **Total A** and the remaining _____ is your net worth.

Are you happy? If not, it may be time for you to focus on investing – see the previous chapter.

BRILL BIT

Once you have completed a bank reconciliation, monthly budget and understand your financial worth it doesn't take long to maintain it each month. It's brilliant to have big financial goals but you must first understand where you are starting from.

PART FOUR
YOUR
RELATIONSHIPS

21

THE RELATIONSHIPS WHEEL

Welcome to the Relationships Wheel. Your relationships with others have a huge impact on your well-being. It is extremely important that you are able to identify good and bad relationships and, in turn, nurture the good relationships and either work on or discard the more challenging ones.

As with every part of this book, we are going to start with an opportunity for you to reflect – this time on relationships with different kinds of people – and give yourself a mark for each type.

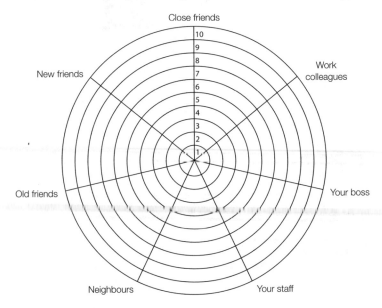

Close friends

So how many do you have? Really close friends, that is, the ones who don't judge, don't ask for anything and seem to have an uncanny knack of knowing when you need them and when they should stay away. Give yourself a point for every genuine one you have.

Now ask yourself what kind of friend you are – always there or a bit too busy? You'd like to be more understanding and give more, but ... Take marks off for the negatives, add some for the positives, then give yourself a score out of 10.

Work colleagues

Are they good friends or simply colleagues? Perhaps you have a mix, but there is 'that one' who drives you nuts. These are often the relationships we can't choose, so they can be difficult at times. If you are in education, think about your class or course mates. Give yourself a low mark if you don't mix well and a higher mark if you make the effort and make it work.

Your boss

So, do you actually talk to your boss or are they someone you avoid at all costs? You don't have to be great friends with your boss to have a good, effective, working relationship where you feel your needs are being met – mutual respect is key here.

Your staff

If you supervise a team, you'll know that managing staff can be one of the most challenging tasks you will ever do. So, as a manager, how is your relationship with your staff? Do you have difficulties relating to them and implementing your ideas? Or do you all work together in a friendly, open and honest way?

If you don't manage staff, give yourself a mark for what type of team member you think you are.

Your neighbours

Do you actually have a connection with your neighbours or are they just a group of people who live close by? If you went next door for a cup of sugar would you be greeted with open arms or a puzzled look of 'who the heck are you?' Give yourself a mark for your relationship with your neighbours.

Old friends

How good are you at staying in touch? Do you remember their birthdays, anniversaries and special occasions? Do you take pride in the fact that you stay in touch? Or can you think of a giant list of old mates whom you haven't seen or spoken to in years?

New friends

How good are you at making new friends? How many new people have you made an effort to meet in the past 12 months and formed new friendships with? Perhaps you have enough friends already and don't need any new ones – lucky you! Or perhaps it's because you're a little shy and fear rejection? If that's you then you have something in common with 90% of other people. Give yourself an honest mark.

Now connect your scores on your Relationships Wheel and take action on the areas where you get a lower mark by turning to the most relevant chapters that follow.

CLOSE FRIENDS

They say you can count your best friends on one hand. You can probably count your 'real' best friends on two thumbs.

When I turned 40 I had a party. I did what I guess everyone does when they have a bash and wrote a list of everyone I wanted to invite. The number became too big, so we looked at ways to reduce it. We began by writing a list of friends we simply couldn't have the party without and we ended up with our final list.

The whole exercise made me reflect on the final invite lists I would make and what kind of friend I am. I'm sure I've let some of my friends down at one time or another and I must rub some people up the wrong way. I do my best to be a good friend as I know all too well what it feels like when friends let us down or don't try as hard as they might.

How to build and keep close friendships

Building and maintaining close, rewarding friendships takes time and involves many shared experiences, but there are some simple tips that will help you along the way:

1 Lower your expectations. We often expect more than people can give for one reason or another and this leads to disappointment. It's much better to focus on what they can give, rather than what we want them or expect them to give.

2 Make the first move. We so often think our friends should be more thoughtful. How about thinking, 'Perhaps it's me who needs to take the first few steps.'

3 Be genuinely interested in what your friends are doing. All too often close friends take each other for granted, thinking they know all there is to know.

4 Don't talk about how wonderful your other friends are when you're with your best friends. Hearing what a brilliant time you had with someone else isn't much fun for a best friend.

5 Write to your friends, even if they live close. One of my wife's best friends, Marion, frequently writes her letters and Christine loves to receive them. They're better than emails.

6   Call for no reason – just for a chat. Try sending a card for no
    reason too – it's amazing how much friends appreciate these
    gestures!

7   Keep your word, avoid cancelling things and show yourself to
    be a reliable loyal friend.

8   Do your best not to judge. Just because someone is your friend
    it doesn't mean you know what is really happening in their lives.
    People without children have no idea what it's like to have
    children until they have their own. You never know what may be
    happening in the background when they are on the phone to
    you and you're recounting your fifth funny story of the day.

9   *Never* lend money to or borrow money from a friend.

Go with the flow

It's a constant endeavour to keep up close friendships and there
are often up times and low times. Try not to make much of the down
times – things will sort themselves out if the friendship is meant to
last.

Don't hold on

Often we grow apart from close friends. It is a sad fact of life, but
you have to be prepared to let close friends go if the relationship is
counterproductive.

Be open

We often close ourselves off to making new close friends. But you'll
be surprised just where and when you might meet someone whom
you can have a lasting and close friendship with – so long as you
are open to this. Your next best friend may be an acquaintance now
who needs just a little encouragement to upgrade to a best mate.
Give them an opportunity!

Final thoughts on best friends

Let them in. Be forgiving and give second chances. Be interested but not too intrusive. Be caring but not overbearing. Be thoughtful but don't meddle. Be fun but know when to be serious. Be giving but don't expect anything in return. And when they let you down (as they will), be understanding. Give them a brilliant reason to become an even better friend to you.

BRILL BIT

Give your best friends amazing presents for birthdays and other special occasions. Many of the gifts they receive may be ill thought out and usually rubbish. Show how much you really care with your thoughtfulness.

23

WORK COLLEAGUES

If you work in an organisation where work colleagues surround you, you'll know just how important it is that you have a good relationship with them. You spend over seven hours a day with them five times a week, supposedly working towards a shared vision. And it's not easy when you didn't necessarily choose to work with these people but you have to face challenges and stressful situations with them on a regular basis. It's not surprising then that when things go wrong with these relationships it can seem like the end of the world and (in some cases) can prevent you from doing your job effectively. So, it really is in your best interests to create good, solid relationships with your colleagues.

How to build brilliant relationships at work

Here are a few things you can do to help your relationships with your work colleagues. Many are office based, so if you're not based in an office environment *think transferable* and decide how they would work best for you.

★ If you are new, cook biscuits and take them in as a 'thank you for making me welcome' present. Don't do this on your first day; no one trusts you yet so you'll be left with a terrible complex (and a tin full of biscuits).

★ Make a massive effort to learn people's names. If you work in a big company make sure you know the most important people's names first (that's security and the cleaners).

★ Make an effort to meet people for lunch. When you do, focus on being interested more than interesting.

★ Now and then, ask about the photographs or anything personal people have on their desks. It shows you have an interest in them beyond their working role.

★ Do your best to understand difficult or miserable colleagues. It may be an opportunity for you to help them with something and will establish you as a trusted member of the team.

★ Meet people outside work – this will give you an all-round perspective of them and a chance to get to know them in a relaxed environment.

Dealing with difficult colleagues

I once worked as a fundraiser for a children's health charity. By the very nature of the project, we attracted some 'interesting' people. The pay wasn't brilliant but the people in the team I got to work with every day were amazing. Then a new person started who (on paper) should have been brilliant – but she wasn't. Not only was she not so good at her job (a polite way of saying she was 'pants') but she infuriated everyone. It was the first time I'd experienced anything like this so I had a chat with my boss. His advice was: 'Just get on with it.' What the heck did that mean? I found myself sitting in a tiny open-plan office with this person who insisted that it had to be 'her way or no way' and on top of that she really thought she was an expert on everything. Not only that but she was loud – very, very loud!

Then one day I had to take a long car journey with her. At 7 am and with my 'just get on with it' hat firmly on, we set off. After an hour had passed she asked a question which really threw me: 'Do you think I'm popular at work?' So, what did I do? ... Of course, I lied. I had to, there were another two hours to travel in the car and three hours back! But I did stumble across a fantastic way to help the journey pass and hopefully make her more bearable. After a couple of minutes, I asked her a question: 'Do *you* think you're popular in the office?' That's when it all came out. She spent 30 minutes telling me how she felt she tried too hard, how she had to push herself forward in her last job, etc. Now I wanted to help her. It was a perfect example of a 'paradigm shift'.

At the end of that busy day she 'thanked me for listening' and I felt good about my support role as an amateur counsellor. I really believed the next day she would come in to the office a changed person, but she didn't. She left shortly afterwards, no one said they missed her and she went to work with the perfect team – herself.

The point of the story is that you will often encounter difficult people at work and sometimes they are simply a bad fit for the team. If this is the case, I'm afraid it's simply a case of riding the storm; but it really pays to take the time, as I did, to get to know them a little better. With a little understanding you can often avoid some unpleasant confrontations.

People like people who are interested rather than people who 'think' they are interesting. Take time to really get to know your colleagues.

24

YOUR BOSS

Having a bad relationship with your boss has a huge impact on your ability to do your job effectively. We look to our bosses for support, appreciation and direction. If this is lacking then there is a huge void in your working life, resulting in a lack of motivation and confidence that may ultimately lead to resignation.

Your relationship with your boss could be complicated by hierarchical levels, politics, targets and measurements, not to mention the new styles of management such as 'matrix' (who's my boss today?) or 'laissez-faire' (who cares who's my boss today?!). Large organisations have multiple layers of management and dozens of bosses; smaller organisations may only have one or two. To this day I don't know which is best.

Manage your boss

No matter how large or small an organisation is, here's something I learned from my second (and best) boss. If your boss is giving you a hard time, it's probably because they are getting a harder time from someone else. If that's true, and you usually won't know for sure, then it makes sense that your boss needs a new manager and that person should be you. I don't mean get your boss's boss's job (unless you really want to – then see the Career Wheel in this book!!); I mean manage them from where you are.

Reality check

Most people think that it's their boss's job to manage them. If you want a brilliant life then you have to learn how to manage your boss – without their knowing it. It's easier than you think and it makes your life and their life better, too.

Eleven tips for managing your boss

1 Work out their type – then play to it!

Lots of companies spend thousands of pounds attempting to profile their staff. Bosses love this as they get to find out 'what type of leader they really are'. Sometimes it's formatted as colours, shapes or even animals that are used to describe their 'predominant style'. As you work for them and live with their 'style', you're qualified to profile them and for half the price! Why do they spend so much money when you could have told them (for the cost of a curry) that they are a 'blue, thruster, antelope with polygon tendencies'? Beats me. It's easy. If they are meticulous, be detailed. If they are colourful – add colour to what you do. The point is that, if your boss has a style, bite your lip and play to it most (not all) of the time and life becomes easier, faster.

2 Help your boss to make decisions

Most bosses don't like making decisions. You may think 'but that's their job' and perhaps you are right. But I know bosses love someone who will say: 'I think we should do xyz and here's why.'

3 Help their memory

In meetings, a quick update of where you left off and the key actions you were working on can be critical to a busy boss. Remember, managing you may account for 10% or less of their time so make it easy for them to get up to speed with you.

4 Be quick to summarise

Bosses are busy. When you get an instruction or are at the end of a meeting, quickly replay the key decisions and your next actions – then get out of there.

5 Know the difference between important and urgent

Sometimes we think we are the only person that our boss should be interested in – especially when something is (in our mind) urgent. It can drive you nuts when they don't appear to be interested in your 'urgent' item – but just stop for a minute and ask how important it is. If it's both high on the importance *and* the urgent ranking then it's time to shout.

6 Be accurate – even if your boss is not

If you have a sloppy boss, the chances are you will be appreciated much more if you focus on being accurate. If you have a precise boss then the same is true. This is one of those unfair rules but it's no excuse saying that they should be more accurate if you don't take the time to be more precise too.

7 Provide clarity

I think I speak for all bosses when I say lack of preparation is one of the most annoying clangers when you are managing a team. This is closely followed by overcomplicated explanations and ill-thought-through plans. The answer is in providing clarity. If you are well prepared and can make complicated ideas and concepts simple, you'll be loved by bosses all your life.

8 Solve it first

I had a boss once who said: 'Don't come to me with problems, come to me with solutions for approval.' When you have a problem and you say to your boss, 'Here's the challenge ... and here's a couple of ways we can deal with it', I guarantee you'll be flavour of the month.

9 Keep it simple

Never assume your boss knows what you are talking about. Technical jargon usually fails to impress, along with the modern management gimmicks you picked up from your last 'offsite'. If you get the feeling you're 'dumbing down' too much, then move up a gear until you're at the same speed as your boss.

10 Take responsibility

Be seen to be open to taking responsibility from your boss and be genuinely open to taking on more responsibility. Bosses have sleepless nights about delegating, so make it easy and you'll quickly find a friendlier side to your boss.

11 Be super trustworthy

I had a colleague who said: 'I don't trust any of my staff, they always let you down.' Don't be 'anyone' – be the one who can be trusted.

It's down to you

Your relationship with your boss is down to you – not them. That can be a bitter pill to swallow, but if you really want to have a brilliant relationship with your boss then it's worth giving these ideas your full attention and action.

BRILL BIT

Don't ever openly criticise your boss. It's too easy to publicly slate a boss for what they did or didn't do. It's a harder road to stay quiet when it seems like everyone else is critical and you have a personal gripe to get off your chest. Say nothing – save it until you get home and, if you have a brilliant listener, tell them – if not, tell your cat.

25

YOUR STAFF

If you find it hard getting on with your boss, try being one! I believe managing staff is one of the most difficult tasks a person ever has to do. I've been working on the right way to manage for many years and I still believe I am a beginner.

Why should it be so hard? All you have to do is find the right people, train them, give clear direction, support them, understand they are human and may make mistakes, allow them flexibility, take the blame if they get it wrong (because you mustn't have briefed them properly), allow them to take the credit when it goes well (to motivate them), ensure you don't break one of the three million employment laws that have been introduced in the last year and pay them a good wage. Come on, it can't be that hard, can it?

Ten tips for managing people

It's a tough job and it's getting tougher all the time. So here are a few ideas to make your life easier.

1 Recruit on values first, then skills

I once had a client whose best salesman got drunk and hit a colleague on a works night out. He was sacked the next day. Even though he was amazing at selling and represented 20% of their annual sales they couldn't keep him as it would have compromised their values. How refreshing! As a boss, if you want to have a brilliant team, it's worth recruiting on people's values first. Skills can be trained in days; values are developed over years. And here's an extra thought. How about throwing potential into the mix, even over experience? Something to think about.

2 Put families first (including yours)

One of our values at Michael Heppell Ltd is 'Family First'. I really enjoy interviewing new staff and explaining what that means. If someone has kids, I'll say: 'Let's imagine it's a school sports day. Don't you dare come and ask me for time off for it!' At this point they usually have a pretty puzzled look on their faces. Then I add: 'We trust you'll be there. As a courtesy to your colleagues, let them know where you'll be, but please don't book official leave as it's expected you'll be there, screaming from the sideline and participating in a parents' race! Is that OK?'

I once had a boss who, when I asked to book time off (having spent a year working 70–80 hours a week) to go to my daughter's sports day, said: 'Michael, your family is starting to get in the way of my business.' I've never found it easier to resign from a job in my life!

Family first is important for your staff but it is *vital* for you. You need to be seen to be living it – don't be a martyr by showing how hard you work at the expense of your family; you'll get more respect by being there for your family, too.

3 Make work fun

Even if you aren't a fun person, have a go! A company I consulted for decided to introduce a 'Dress-down Friday'. Their chief operations officer arrived wearing a pair of golfing trousers, a 100% polyester tee-shirt, white socks and open-toed sandals. Everyone giggled as he was the most boring member of the management team. It was only at 10.30, when an urgent email from the chief exec arrived appealing for everyone to stop mentioning how funny Alan looked, that the staff realised he wasn't in fancy dress. His wardrobe consisted of suits for work (and home), golf gear and terrible holiday clothes. Ouch!

The point is he had a go and because he did, it helped to loosen everyone up. The giggles soon diminished and Alan showed another side to his personality.

4 Forgive quickly

When a member of your team does let you down, and they will, don't hold a grudge. Nine times out of 10 they'll be feeling a lot worse about the situation than you think, and moving on and being positive is just what may be needed.

5 Educate yourself

How much time do you spend learning how to be a better leader? How many courses have you invested in? How many books have you read? How much time have you spent with a leadership coach? If you want to get better you need to invest in yourself.

6 Don't use your 'profile' as an excuse

'I'm an "ideas person" so I'll just need to think of ideas for you to carry out.' Yes, I actually heard a person say that to their team after receiving their 'profile' from a facilitator just 24 hours earlier. Happy team? What do you think?

Don't make your weaknesses an excuse.

7 Let your staff know bad news quickly

If something isn't right, you can be sure your team intuitively know about it faster than you thought they would. By letting your team know quickly that there is a challenge and that either 'you are working on it' or 'they can help by ...' you'll build trust and be surprised how willing your team are to help.

8 Delegate then abdicate

Many bosses want to delegate but few want to abdicate. That's why once they've delegated they dabble, interfere and eventually sicken the person they delegated to. Then they love to take it back with a sense of 'I knew no one could do this as well as me'. It's tough, but by truly learning how to delegate not only will you become a far better leader but you will empower an amazing team to support you.

9 Use your intuition

If it feels wrong, it probably is. Many bosses stop using their intuition the second they are given a team to manage. So, the next time a member of your team 'seems' unhappy, they probably are. The next time a situation 'feels' awkward, it usually is. The next time you 'sense' you aren't doing a brilliant job, it's because you're not.

10 Have brilliant manners

Good afternoon, good morning, please and thank you. Give some eye contact and genuinely listen. It's not rocket science but if you're not making an effort to do it every day then people will have noticed. The good news is it takes a day to fix.

You have been given a great responsibility to be a boss. In years to come do you want people to look back and say: 'I had this boss once, they were hard but fair, they really listened to me, they helped with my personal and professional development and when the time came for me to move on they were so supportive. They were amazing.' Or do you want them to say: 'I worked for this person once who thought they were a great boss but, actually, they were a bit of a prat.'

Your choice.

BRILL BIT

In your role as a boss you will probably have more impact on an individual's development than any other person in their life (other than their parents or possibly partners). What a wonderful obligation – please take it seriously.

26

YOUR
NEIGHBOURS

A few good neighbours are worth their weight in gold. It's great to have someone to chat to, to do little favours for, and to be able to ask for help in return. And all on your doorstep (literally). If you've ever had a strained relationship with a neighbour, you'll know what a negative impact that can have on your life – and it's not easy to avoid somebody who lives right outside your house.

I've always had good neighbours. Is that because I'm lucky or because I've worked hard to be a good neighbour? Something to think about.

I live in a small village where most people know each other. But even when I've lived in a town or a terrace I've always made sure I introduced myself to my neighbours, was extremely polite and worked hard at fitting into the community.

Building neighbourly respect

You don't have to be best mates with your neighbours; in most cases you didn't choose them; however, there is a level of respect that is needed to be a good neighbour.

You may be thinking: 'Well, if they were more respectful to me then I would reciprocate.' Perhaps you have problem neighbours or they are just too 'different'. Here are a few techniques to help. They are designed to help you take down the barricades, build a bridge or in some cases make the move from neighbours to buddies:

★ **The smile and wave.** When you see a neighbour, give them a big smile with a small half-moon wave. Do this a few times until you build trust.*

★ **Hello.** The next step is a simple and easy one. Come on, it's not like you've forgotten the words! Just say 'Hello'.

★ **Meaningless greetings.** 'Nice day', 'Horrible day', 'Looks like it might rain' or any other weather-related nonsense goes down well. Just get past hello and say something more.

★ **Hi, I'm ...** A bit more daring and should only be attempted by the brave and fearless or after completing all the above. Yes, it's time to introduce yourself. Here's how. 'Hi, I'm Michael, I've

*Not all on the same occasion; that would make you look slightly mad!

lived here for x weeks, months, years and I've just realised I
don't know your name.'

At this point, if they don't want to speak, you can rest easy knowing
you did all you could to build a neighbourly friendship.

There's more to being a good neighbour than a wave and a smile

Being a good neighbour is about other things, too. Here are some
things you can do to be a better neighbour:

★ Take your neighbour's bin out if they've forgotten.

★ Bring it back in later.

★ Push any papers left hanging out of their letterbox right
through.

★ Check on their house or car if their alarm goes off.

★ Send your neighbours a Christmas card.

★ If you share grass, cut their side too.

★ Repair both fences.

★ Keep the noise down.

★ Let them know if you are going to be away.

I'm making the assumption that you'll apply good sense to all of the
above points, i.e. avoid letting your neighbour know if you are going
to be away if he is called Mr Raffles. But give as many as you can
a go and see what happens.

Reality check

So what if you do have the neighbours from hell or you fall out with
people just a few yards away? There's a lot to be said for being
dignified, especially when the temptation is to scream! Deep
breaths, a simple nod as you pass and then just get on with your
life. You'll only see them for a fraction of your day so don't allow
them to put you off living a full and happy life.

Sign for a parcel if a neighbour isn't in and deliver it to them as soon as they get home. Hand it over the way you'd like a delivery person to hand it to you.

OLD FRIENDS

Lea McConnell is one of my oldest friends; he's been in my life forever. I think we went to the same nursery and I'm certain we went to the same infant and junior schools. I know that because, when he wasn't at my house for tea, I was at his. We went through school together and then at 16 we went our separate ways. We saw each other now and then. Unfortunately, the 'now and then' has stretched to every five years or more. How did that happen?

What about all those people I've worked with over the years that I said 'let's stay in touch' to – but never did. Then there are the people you meet on courses, your neighbours, pub pals, holiday friendships and family friends. As I'm writing this, I've realised how rubbish I am at staying in touch with old friends. So, if you are an old friend of mine, make it easy for me and get in touch!

How to stay in touch

The fact is, it's easy to keep in touch with old friends. It requires little effort and is a great way of keeping connected to important parts of our past. Here are some tips for me (and you!) to take action and contact our old friends:

★ Register for some online networking; from Facebook to LinkedIn there are plenty of ways to find people.

★ Once you find them, CONTACT THEM. It's lovely to see old friends on screen but what's the point unless you are going to get in touch?

★ Go through old address books and call one person a week.

★ Take your old address books on holiday and send lots of postcards.

★ Go to reunions if you are invited. Or at least contact the people you'd like to see most and see if they are going.

What to say after all those years

So, what do you say to an old friend? When Louise (a friend we made on holiday 10 years earlier) called us last summer she simply said: 'Hi, it's Louise, I've been meaning to give you a call for months.' We talked for ages about kids, life and everything. It was lovely.

Here are a couple of other 'openers':

★ 'Hi, it's _____ do you remember me? You've popped into my head a few times recently so I thought I'd give you a call.'

★ 'Hi, it's _____ I'm reading a fantastic book called *How to Have a Brilliant Life* and in it the author challenges you to contact an old friend. I thought of you, so here I am!'

BRILL BIT

It can be the case that the people who were with you when you went from 'a to b' are not necessarily the right people to be with you from 'b to c'. That's OK; feeling guilty because you haven't been in touch with a person who isn't right for you now is nothing to be concerned about – in fact, not staying in touch could be the best decision you've made.

28

NEW FRIENDS

What if I said I'll be your friend? In fact, I'll be a brilliant friend. I'll call just the right amount of times and I'll always do what I promise. I'll guarantee to remember your birthday and buy you an imaginative gift that you'll actually like. Of course, I'll be there for you when times are tough and I'll be hilariously funny, but never at your expense. Oh yes, one more thing, I'll be really focused on making you look good even if I have to sit quietly and let you be the centre of attention.

Who'd like a friend like that? Everyone! And I think you've worked out what's coming next – it's YOU who needs to think and be like that if you want to make some brilliant new friends.

Finding friends

Finding new friends can seem like a daunting task. If you don't have many friends, it's easy to feel very isolated and not know how to make a start. But it's actually very simple; you just have to be proactive about it – so, don't wait at home for them to find you! Here's something to get you started.

My challenge to you is this: have a conversation with one stranger a day for the next five days. This is not to find new friends, so it can be anyone. Taxi drivers, people on the bus, standing in a queue, in the supermarket – anyone. It's about giving you the confidence to talk to new people.

After you've done this for five days, you should be feeling more relaxed about talking to strangers. Next start conversations again, but this time keep talking for over 10 minutes. It may seem like a long time, but this is a must, even if it turns out to be a terrible conversation; it's all part of the process.

The art of conversation

Once you've managed this, think about how you approach conversation. Be open and try to say 'yes' more often. One of the loveliest people I've met must be Danny Wallace, who wrote a brilliant book called *Yes Man*. In it, he describes how his life changes because he was challenged to say 'yes' more often. He replied to weird invitations, visited places he would never have dreamed of and, in the end … Well, you have to read the book, but let's put it this way, he made some brilliant new friends.

Once you start to meet people, be interested in them rather than trying to be interesting. When we meet people for the first time there seems to be a huge amount of pressure for us to impress. The secret is to change the focus from trying to make an impression to making them feel special.

Plan to see them again

The key to making friends is to see a person more than once. Stupidly obvious but this is a point where some people feel uncomfortable right at the critical moment. Remember we're making friends; this is not a guide to dating, so the key is to have been interesting enough for that person to want to spend time with you again. If they do, great; if not, next! There are thousands of people out there who want to make friends – with you!

There are lots of people who also need to make new friends

Don't think of yourself as the only person who finds it hard to make new friends. There are lots of reasons why you might be reading this now; perhaps you have just moved in to a new area, maybe you have just ended a relationship or you have been caring for a family member. Whatever your experience, I would imagine there are other people who are in your area who have had a similar experience, too.

People like people who are like themselves

These days there are groups and clubs for every situation, interest, hobby or belief you can imagine. What a great place to meet like-minded people. Go to your library and start asking questions about your interest, join a club and show up.

Final thought. Don't be too needy. No one likes a person who is too desperate to make friends. They get the impression their new buddy is going to be hard work. It's a close call sometimes but, if in doubt, ask your intuition. Your intuition knows you pretty well by now – it's been with you all your life, so if it's shouting 'back off' then take heed.

BRILL BIT

Tell yourself that you are a brilliant friend and you are currently auditioning for new ones. By internally repeating that you are a brilliant friend you'll feel confident, relax more and attract the right people into your life.

PART FIVE
YOUR
CONTRIBUTION

29

THE
CONTRIBUTION
(AND HIGHER
PURPOSE) WHEEL

This wheel is split into two halves that perfectly complement each other. The first is based on your levels of contribution, the second covers your higher purpose.

As you score yourself, be very honest with your responses, as the scores you give here may bring up some interesting questions or even give you a missing link on how to achieve your brilliant life.

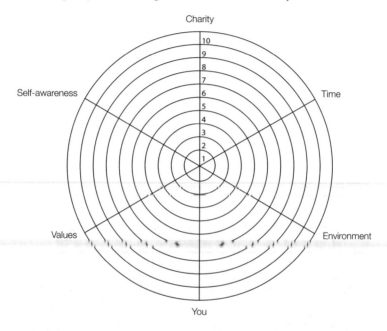

Charity

Before you give yourself a mark, this is charity in its widest sense, so look at everything you give that may be for a charitable purpose. As always, you are measuring your own gut feeling. For some, putting a pound in a charity box may score a high mark; for others, major donations or organising spectacular events and volunteering 20 hours a week may still feel like you've not done enough.

Give yourself an honest mark on your charitable endeavours.

Your time

Do you give your time freely? Are you prepared to go an extra mile to help out those whose need it or are you chasing your tail just trying to get the basics right for you?

Your belief may be that if you had more time then you would contribute more. But often it's the people with the most already on their life plate who give time to others. So, be honest and give yourself a mark for your contribution of time.

The environment

From recycling to reducing your carbon footprint, from tidying rubbish in your street to making an impact on people's thinking, how do you rate yourself on a scale of 1 to 10 for your contribution to your environment?

You

How much of you are you happy to share? From your ideas to a pint of blood, how happy are you to share yourself, your most precious possession? Are you happy to get involved with your local community or share your knowledge to make things better? If so, then give yourself a high mark. If you have your list of excuses all lined up, then, sorry, your mark has to be lower.

Your values

Are you values driven? Or are you swayed by the crowd and popular beliefs? Would you be happy to stand up for something you believed in even though it might not be a popular choice? Could you immediately write your top 10 values and why you have them?

Give yourself an honest mark for this vital part of life.

Self-awareness

Who are you? How aware are you of what makes you tick? Do you know your definite purpose? Do you allow yourself to be your authentic self? Or are you just getting by each day, still trying to work it all out?

If you are highly aware, then you can give yourself a high mark; if you're not or you don't know what on earth I'm talking about, then give yourself a lower mark and read the self-awareness section.

Now join up the scores and turn to the sections where you need some help.

CHARITY

One of the major challenges faced by people who want to be more charitable is that they don't know how. The closest we get to education on how to give tends to come from non-uniform days at school or national televised appeals twice a year. Yet there is so much more.

Here are seven big and small things you could do to give yourself one of the best feelings in the world by supporting a charitable cause.

Volunteer some time every week for 90 days

People often don't volunteer because they are worried they have to make a lifetime commitment. Guess what? You don't! Many organisations would love to have a regular contribution of your time over the next 90 days. Just 3 hours a week equates to 36 hours in a 90-day period! Don't think about it as volunteering; think more as if you are offering to help for a bit.

Raise some serious money

Any amount of money is brilliant to raise but why not go for raising some serious cash for a cause close to your heart?

I was a professional fundraiser for five years and during that time I would see one person's coffee morning raise £15 and another's raise £150. How? It was nothing to do with the people they were attracting; it was more to do with focus. Some people used a charity fundraiser as an opportunity to have a good time and if they raised some money then that was a bonus. Others focused on raising the most money possible while also having a good time. So, go for it! Set yourself a 90-day target and see what you can achieve.

Support core running costs

For charities, it's much easier to fundraise for the sexy stuff than for core running costs and salaries. Fuelled by dramatists, some people are led to believe charity running costs are too high. Some may be, but most aren't. So, why not make a donation just to support the day-to-day costs?

Create leverage

One of the best ways to get maximum benefit from your donation is to see whether your donation will have a potential effect far bigger than simply what it will buy.

A relatively small donation to a campaigning group in a small town in California gave them the funds they needed to launch an initiative to encourage local schools to buy locally grown organic fruit and vegetables. This then led to a county-wide initiative and, currently, a state proposal. Tens of thousands of young people are eating healthier food, local organic farmers are feeling the benefits and a major change has occurred. All because one person identified the key entry point.

Investing in the development of leadership in organisations is another powerful way to do this.

Give your expertise

You probably have some specific skills that a charity would appreciate. You'll be amazed at how grateful people will be if you give your expertise. For more ideas, see Chapter 33.

Here's an extra thought. When you do give your expertise, only take it as far as the people you are helping want you to take it. You want to be known as a 'Brilliant helpful person' – not 'That pain who wanted to change everything'.

Get it on the family agenda

Do you spend time as a family discussing the type of charity you want to support and how? Why not ask each member of your family to research one organisation they would like to support, then bring their findings to the table and discuss them? What could be better than spending time over a family meal discussing the causes you are interested in and how you can help them?

Give a major personal donation

I know there are people reading this book who can afford to give a major gift and just haven't got round to it yet. Why? It's usually because people don't know 'who to give it to', 'how much to give' or think they 'can't give enough'.

Did you know that more money is given to charity (as a percentage of wealth) by poorer people in the UK? As Salvatore LaSpada* of the UK-based Institute for Philanthropy says: 'Philanthropy is the domain of the poor.' You don't need to be a billionaire to be a philanthropist!

Take a look at **www.guidestar.org.uk**, which lists thousands of charities in the UK.

How much to give? A major gift should be enough so you feel a little 'financial pain' but not so much that you won't want to do it again.

For more advice on large-gift donations, and other areas of philanthropy, visit **www.instituteforphilanthropy.org.uk**.

Something everyone can do

★ You know when you stay in a hotel and they give you those little bottles of shampoo and stuff in the bathroom? Try not to use them; instead, collect as many as you can and drop them off at a homeless shelter.

---

*Thank you to Salvatore LaSpada of the Institute for Philanthropy for his help with this section.

* Buy the *Big Issue* and, if you don't want to read it, give it back to the seller so they can sell it again.
* Write a letter for Amnesty International. Visit **www.amnesty.org** to find out how. (I just did it, found a cause I supported and wrote a letter – it took me six minutes.)
* Instead of trying to look skyward so you don't catch their eye, give some spare change (or at least a smile) the next time you are asked.
* Help an elderly person across the road. (Best to ask if they actually want to cross the road first!)
* Give decent clothes to a charity shop. They'll be grateful for anything but before you hand it over ask 'Is this wearable?' If you buy something from a charity shop insist on giving them more than they ask – it's called reverse haggling and it's a hoot!
* The next time you see a person with a collecting tin give them all your change and encourage your mates to do the same thing. Then thank the collector profusely for their hard work.

How many times to give?

When I was a kid my Dad taught me a brilliant lesson about giving to charity. It was close to Christmas and the local Salvation Army brass band was playing in the main street of our town. As he walked past, my Dad put some money in the tin. Mum and Dad then went to the supermarket to do the weekly 'big shop'. About an hour later they left laden with bags and there (now in the supermarket car park) was the Salvation Army band, still playing carols. Right on cue a cheery lady with a tin waved it in front of my parents. Once again, Dad made a donation.

That night sitting at home watching TV they heard the sounds of *Hark the Herald Angels Sing* drifting down their street. You guessed it, the Salvation Army band. A few minutes later there was a knock on the door. My Dad jumped up and was greeted by another Salvation Army volunteer with a tin. Once again, he happily made a donation.

> Returning to his comfy sofa, my Mum said: 'Why didn't you tell her you'd already given to them twice today?'
>
> Dad said: 'I would hope that if someone needed shelter on a bitterly cold evening like tonight the Salvation Army wouldn't say, "You've already been here twice."'

When it comes to charity, don't expect the government to fund everything. Park your cynicism. Give a little more than you planned. Make it tax efficient (charities get lots more that way). Educate yourself about giving and the impact you can make. Keep on doing it!

31

YOUR TIME

How much time do you contribute? Actually, let me rephrase that. How much time do you contribute *without expecting anything in return*?

Most people would be happy to give more time if they got more for it. The idea of contributing time can be a daunting challenge for many people because they already feel they don't have enough for themselves.

How much time is enough?

Enough to: watch the news? Read a paper? Catch up on some gossip? You can see where I'm going.

'Hands up who's got too much time?' That's a question I accidentally asked a group of category B prison inmates (I was in flow!) while working on a 'How to Be Brilliant' programme for repeat offenders. I'd asked the question so many times, to so many audiences and it just slipped out. Of course, all their hands went up and I had to spend the next 30 minutes listening to their stories of parole panels and criminal injustice.

So, let me ask you. Do you have too much time? Most people have this belief. 'If I had more time than I would contribute more time.' Unfortunately, that paradox means that they'll never give more, as everyone has the same amount of time – it's just how we choose to use it.

Choosing how to use your time

And that's the key word – how you *choose* to use it. It's much more about a mindset that you want to give some (or some more) of your time rather than whether you have enough. Once you realise that it is about choice, you can elevate your thinking into decision mode.

Extra hours

Here's a fun game to play.

You are given an extra hour every day (lucky you – the 25-hour day). What are you going to do with it? Look at the list below and say the first choice that comes to mind:

★ Stay in bed or go to work?

★ Cook a meal or take some exercise?

★ Watch TV or read a book?

★ Make love or make the beds?

★ Try something new or look at old photographs?

★ Volunteer or get an early night?

★ Call two friends or write to one?

★ Surf the net or clean your shoes?

There are no right or wrong answers; however, if you have answered honestly you'll begin to see what you prioritise and give your time to in your busy life. This is a brilliant game to play with your partner, family or a group of friends. Remember to go back and ask 'why?' after the answers.

A time challenge

My challenge to you is this. If you made a decision right now to contribute 3 hours a week for 12 weeks to something other than you, without needing any recognition or financial reward, could you do it?

If the answer was yes, then my next challenge to you is to find a way to make it happen.

If it was no, then take a long hard look in the mirror and ask yourself 'why'? And keep on asking 'why' until you get to the truth.

How would you like three extra hours a week?

Here's another challenge. If I could show you a way to gain those three hours a week would you contribute them to doing something for others? If so, read on for my ...

Top 10 tips to save 30 minutes a day and still have a lie-in on Sunday

1 Go to bed 15 minutes later and get up 15 minutes earlier! Too hard? OK, read on, there are nine more for lazybones.

2 Learn the right way to say 'no'. My friend uses this: 'I'd love to [add what it is you've been asked to do] but I promised myself something. This year if I'm going to do something, I'm only going to do it if I know I can give it 100% and I'm concerned that I can't give this 100%, so thank you for asking but no.' It works and most people give him his space.

3 Have a big clear out. Junk slows you down.

4 Only check your emails twice a day.

5 Don't watch the news.

6 Time phone calls and give yourself mental challenges for how long you'll talk.

7 Move faster, walk faster and talk faster.

8 Book 45-minute meetings instead of hour-long ones.

9 Learn how to delegate.

10 Buy in some help.

If you test out all these 10 tips, you are bound to save at least half an hour a day or even more; loads more timesaving tips can be found at **www.saveanhour.co.uk**. Contribute this time – the rewards are amazing.

BRILL BIT

Volunteer some time with a friend or a group of friends. You are much more likely to see it through and you'll be able to share your experiences with some special people.

32

THE ENVIRONMENT

More has been written on the environment in the past five years than in the previous 50. The main reason is because we now know that we (me and you) need to be responsible and we can't rely on anyone other than ourselves to do something about it.

Researching this section I noticed there was a lot of information from pre-2000 about how we are damaging the environment in which we live. What struck me most now is the increased speed we are doing it at.

And I'm not talking about melting ice caps or deforesting areas the size of Wales. This is about our local, national and international environment. Here's the good news; there's loads you can do to make a positive impact.

Here are 50 big and small things you can do

If you can tick 40 you are well on your way to making a positive impact:

1   Turn the tap off while you brush your teeth.

2   Recycle your glass, cardboard, plastic – everything your council allows you to.

3   Repair before you renew.

4   Accelerate slowly.

5   Change your light bulbs for energy-efficient ones.

6   Insulate – everything.

7   Plant some trees (there are organisations that will help you do this).

8   Pick up local litter.

9   Walk.

10   Make something with leftovers.

11   Let nature do its thing.

12 Ask your power supplier for advice on how to save.

13 Wash clothes on a lower temperature.

14 Fit a solar panel.

15 Use one less sheet of loo paper for every sitting.

16 Cancel unwanted 'junk' mail through the Mailing Preference Service.

17 Buy local produce.

18 Switch your lights off.

19 Turn your thermostat down by a degree.

20 Don't leave TVs, etc. on standby.

21 Report fly tipping.

22 Grow your own vegetables.

23 Catch a train.

24 Buy Fairtrade.

25 Use a cup or glass for your water or coffee-vending machine instead of plastic.

26 Take your own bags to the supermarket.

27 Recycle your old mobile phone (**www.fonebak.com**).

28 Dispose of chewing gum carefully.

29 Only fill the kettle with what you need.

30 Recycle spectacles (**www.vao.org.uk**).

31 Build up your tolerance and turn the air conditioning off.

32 Use paper on both sides.

33 Use a pen until it runs out of ink.

34 Tidy your garden.

35 Discuss this list with your kids (easy).

36 Discuss this list with your parents (harder?).

37 Don't watch TV in bed.

38 Find someone who works near you and give them a lift.

39 Unplug your mobile phone as soon as it is charged.

40 Don't print it unless you really, really need to.

41 Dog owners – pick up your dog's poo.

42 Organise a litter pick.

43 Peg your washing out instead of tumble drying.

44 Create your own compost heap.

45 Turn your computer screen off.

46 Before you throw away see if you can give away first.

47 Have lots of plants in your house.

48 Turn off 'background' TV.

49 Allow part of your garden to grow wild.

50 Feed the birds in winter.

It's interesting that everything we do to 'save' the planet for the future also just happens to make the planet a more beautiful place to live on now. So, what are you waiting for? It's time for you to make a positive impact on the environment and, even though your actions may seem small, in the scheme of things they will equal big marks on your environmental score in your Contribution Wheel.

BRILL BIT

Teach small children about the importance of environmental contribution. Then teach the bigger ones (like you).

33

YOU

While you have been reading I've found out something about you. You are an amazing, wonderful unique individual. You can do things the rest of us could only dream of doing. You can think vast thoughts, do grand things and achieve greatness. You're brilliant, you are! Is there any chance of you sharing some of that brilliance?

Most people at some time in their lives look at others and think, 'If I had what they had then I'd do more.'

The point is, people have looked at *you* and thought that.

Here are two stories of people who found how to give a bit of 'you'.

Carole, the talking book

Carole was 63 before she realised she had an amazing skill. All through her life Carole was happy to play small: in her marriage, as a mother and in her job, she 'just got on with it'. When her husband had a stroke he lost his sight in one eye and most of the sight in the other. She looked after him and used to spend hours reading him books.

A year after his stroke Carole's husband spent a week in a local respite care home – to give her a rest. While he was there, Carole went in to visit him and would read a few chapters of a book. On the second visit, Carole was amazed to find more than a dozen people waiting to hear her read. They had been 'listening in' to her vivid reading during her last visit and wanted to hear more. By the end of the week, Carole was reading to 30 people. 'Better than a radio play', 'I love the different voices', 'The way she reads it's like you're there', were some of the comments.

Then requests came in. Would Carole read to the residents once or twice a week? Then via a friend of a friend would she visit another home for the elderly? That was five years ago. Even though her husband has now passed away Carole keeps on reading three or four times a week using her skill to bring joy to others.

Ric burgers

Ric cooked, in his own words, 'the greatest burger on the planet'. He would regularly make 20 and bring them to work. Everyone loved Ric's burgers. But his best burgers were appreciated one cold Saturday night after he'd contacted a local charity supporting homeless people and offered to cook 'Ric burgers' for everyone. Over 200 burgers were grilled that night.

Ric told me: 'They get loads of people who want to help out at Christmas time but not so many in the middle of February when it's so cold your tomato sauce is freezing. It's the most amazing thing to do, to share my burgers.'

What skills do you have? Here's a checklist to see what parts of the 'brilliant you' you can contribute:

Energy	Fun	Cooking
Enthusiasm	Strength	Patience
Organisational skills	Time during the day	Understanding of teenagers
Typing	A steady hand	Creativity
IT skills	A van	A musical talent
Humour	Specialist knowledge	Understanding of accounts
Love of animals	Business sense	Writing
A trade	A pint of blood?*	Excellent contacts
Design skills		

BRILL BIT

Learn how to save a life. Do a first-aid course. It only takes a few hours. Imagine how it would feel if you were ever called on to use those skills – and could!

*We all have spare blood and most people can give some. It takes less than an hour, it's extremely rewarding and right now there is a shortage. If it's something you have been meaning to do, then go online, find your nearest session and schedule it in your diary.

34

YOUR VALUES

n my first book, *How to Be Brilliant*, I described values as being right up there with oxygen. Meaning if you get your values right life is easy; get them wrong and you're in trouble.

Values are the classic subconsciously 'learned behaviour'. We aren't born with them, we rarely sit down and plan what they should be, we just acquire them. And that's the danger.

Having a set of values that you 'just picked up' is fine if the people who are teaching you those values (by their behaviours) are positive role models. But what if they're not? Or, even more dangerous, what if you think they are but they're not?

Your values make you who you are

During a training programme, part of which taught attendees how to identify core values, a participant revealed he had a list that included 'passion', 'winning', 'success', 'power', 'achievement', 'being best' and 'obsession'.

The next stage of the exercise was to write a description of the person you would ultimately want to become – what you wanted to be remembered for. His list included 'compassionate', 'healthy', 'loving', 'understanding', 'generous' and 'relaxed'. Slight values clash? What do you think?

How to write and live with positive rewarding values

So, here's the exercise.

Step one: Make a list of your current values. Here's a list to help you get started; select the ones that honestly describe you and then add your own:

Success	Fun	Passion
Greed	Enthusiasm	Power
Love	Health	Honesty
Recognition	Control	Jealousy

Excitement	Blame	Security
Contribution	Creativity	Fame
Worry	Acceptance	

Step two: Write a description of the type of person you ultimately want to become. Ask yourself if the first list represents the values of the person you ultimately want to become. If it's a 'yes', then that's easy; just keep on doing what you are doing. If it's a 'no' or a 'maybe' then ask yourself: 'What are the values of the person I want to become?' Then when you have this list, simply live your life to those values and you'll become that person.

Sounds too easy? Most of us aren't conscious of our values. They tend to exist at a subconscious level, which means that we don't spot the challenges when they sneak up on us.

Here's an example. Perhaps one of your values is 'jealousy'. Whoa, wait a minute, can that be a value? Do you look at what other people have and feel jealous? If you do that on a regular basis, then that's a value. I know it may seem like a negative one, but nevertheless it *is* a value (a behaviour that you keep repeating). So, if you then look at your description of the person you ultimately want to become and there's no hint of a person who is jealous – what next?

It's time to reprogramme. In order to reprogramme your values you have to hold them in your conscious mind. One of the best ways to do this is to write them down. If you can, create a small laminated card with your values printed on. Use this as your reference.

What to do when you catch yourself using a negative value

When you catch yourself using a negative value, one you don't want to be associated with, take out your card and find a value that is the opposite of the negative one you have just felt. For example, let's go back to jealousy. You catch yourself being unnecessarily jealous of a friend's new car and rather than sharing their excitement you find you are having thoughts along the lines of: 'How did they afford that?' 'I should have a car like that', etc. Remember your 'new' values list, then select a positive value for this occasion. It may be something like 'generous'. So, be generous with your excitement, be generous with your praise, be generous with your compliments.

Here's the exciting part. You can very quickly eliminate jealousy and replace it with more positive values. As with any technique it works best if you throw yourself into it, believe it's going to work and keep at it.

BRILL BIT

Once you have written your values and the description of the person you ultimately want to become, read it every morning and every night. You will create an amazing positive energy which will help you to live those values every day.

SELF-AWARENESS

Who are you and what are you here to do? Do you know? Have you ever asked yourself? If so, what have you discovered?

A tortoise and a hare were having a pint one day when the tortoise (who appeared to have had one too many) challenged the hare to a game of darts. The whole forest came out to watch and, as it happens, the hare thrashed the tortoise. Because, as we all know, tortoises can't play darts.

Hands up who after the first few words thought the last paragraph was going to be the traditional story of the tortoise and the hare? Even when I got into it, I bet you still thought the tortoise was going to win. That's the story we've been told and the outcome we expect.

So, what stories are you telling yourself and which outcomes are you expecting? By telling yourself the same old story you'll get the same old results.

Thinking about nothing

A few years ago I was introduced to top coach, Peter Field. Peter agreed to take me on as a client and I was very excited to have such an amazing person to coach me.

One of my homework tasks was to spend time every day thinking about … nothing. I'm normally processing around 2000 ideas a minute, reflecting on the past, planning the future and working out what I'm going to say and do next. So, the idea of thinking about nothing, even for a minute, was daunting.

Just try it right now. Close your eyes, take three deep breaths and think of nothing. Just for a minute.

How did you do? As my son would say, 'It's rock' (that means difficult by the way).

Impossible tasks

The next time we met, I asked Peter why he'd asked me to do such an impossible task. He suggested that it wasn't impossible; I just believed it was impossible for me.

Well, that was it, the challenge was on. Another month went by and another month of 'failing' ensued. By now I felt like Daniel in the *Karate Kid*, but at least after three months he knew how to 'wax on, wax off' and 'paint the fence'!

At our next meeting Peter revealed that the exercise had been part of the preparation for my next task – to focus on me.

Self-awareness, mindfulness, being connected. Whatever you want to call it is fine, but taking time to actually do it is the challenge. It's one of those classic self-development tools that could be described as simple but not easy. However, it's worth testing and perfecting as the feeling of calm and really being in the moment is amazing.

How to start the search

I've met many people who are searching for their true self. I've met many people who don't even know there's such a thing and I've met a few, very few, who have found it.

Here's a simple guide to becoming more self-aware:

★ Wake up a little earlier, get ready and practise 15 minutes' silent meditation. If you want to, aim to think of nothing or just focus on only one thing.

★ Think about what you do and why you do it. Don't judge yourself but every time you make a discovery tell yourself: 'Isn't that interesting.'

★ Be grateful for everything you have now. You have attracted everything you have. That means you can keep it or release it.

★ Be better for yourself first.

★ Get a coach who can take you through this process. It's one of the most enlightening things you will ever do.

The most interesting element of exploring self-awareness is how effortless it becomes. Higher self-awareness is a state of mind and like any state it can be affected by many things: the people you spend time with, the work you do, your own destructive thoughts and the input of a thousand other variables.

Keep working at it: you'll get your breakthrough and the next time you do your Contribution Wheel you'll be able to give yourself a brilliant mark for self-awareness.

BRILL BIT

Becoming self-aware does not mean becoming selfish.

PART SIX
YOUR VISION

THE VISION WHEEL

Your future. Is it in your hands or are you letting it slip away? Let's see.

Know what you want

It's difficult to have a vision if you don't know what you want. Give yourself an honest mark from 1 to 10 for your certainty that you know what you want. Knowing exactly gives you a 10, 'haven't got a clue' gives you a 1.

Short-term vision (the next 90 days)

Do you have your weeks planned out? Do you know what your vision looks like for the short term or for the next 7, 30 and 90 days with a plan on how you are going to achieve it? Then, well done! It's high short-term vision marks for you. If you can't get past Friday then I think you know how to mark this one.

Medium-term vision (1–5 years)

Can you see yourself in a couple of years? Are you moving on up or is the future static? What do you see as your key projects for the next few years and how will you achieve them? If you aren't sure how well you are doing in this area, then take a look back at your past few years and see how many of your goals you have achieved.

Long-term vision (5+ years)

It's the big one! Can you see yourself in 10 years' time? Do you know what you will be doing? Do you have a plan of how you will achieve it? Who will be with you? How many lives will you positively affect on the way?

   If you have clarity for your long-term vision, give yourself a high mark. Not so sure? Then you lose a few points and if you dare to think 'well if I win the lottery …' you *lose five marks*!

Written plans

So, even if you have short-, medium- and long-term visions, do you have a written plan for how you will achieve them? You get a few points if you make notes in a diary or planner, more if you consciously take time to write your plans, and full marks if you have a document that lists your visions, has images of each one and a separate individual written plan for how you will achieve them.

Visualisation

Can you see it, feel it, smell it, hear it and touch it? Or do you close your eyes and just see darkness? Can you convince your nagging negative mind that you will achieve and fulfil your vision or does the wedge of doubt start to take over?

Resources

Do you have everything you need to ensure your vision becomes a reality? Do you have the right people around you? Have you the education you need or the time required? By having the correct resources your vision becomes a reality faster and more effectively. Are your resources in place? Give yourself a mark.

Now join up the scores and you'll have a clearer picture of where you are with your Vision Wheel.

KNOW WHAT YOU WANT

Tell me what you want. What you really, *really* want. (Hey, that could almost work as a lyric!)

Most people know what they *don't* want: 'I don't want to be lonely', 'I don't want to be ill', 'I don't want to be fat', but ask them what they *do* want and you'll be deafened by the silence.

When I teach my goal-setting workshop, I start by asking people to write down 50 things they want. I'm amazed that most people's lists dry up after a handful of ideas, so I start giving all sorts of suggestions from the minute to the massive. Then I see people writing with a glint in their eye.

Could you write down 50 things that you want?

Don't worry, you won't have to go for them all, but could you brainstorm 50?

Have a go yourself first, then, if you got stuck, here are some to get you restarted:

Get fit	Holiday in Italy
Write a book	Drive a _____ (add your fave car here)
Paint	Eat at a Michelin starred restaurant
Fly first class	Win an award
Have children	Drink champagne on a yacht
Go for more walks	Find a fulfilling career
Get a nose job	Learn to speak French
Meet your hero	Ride a motorcycle
Quit smoking	Build your own website
Learn to play bass	Find a cure for something
Read all the books you own	Sing in public
Own your own house	Start yoga classes
Train your dog	Graduate from university
Be debt free	Take up photography
Fly a kite	Learn how to dance

Scuba dive	Be medication free
Climb a rock wall	Hike in Nepal
Learn karate	Get a PhD
Write music	Write songs
Complete an Ironman	Get an A in something
Do 100 situps a day	Learn origami
Hang glide	Double your salary
Tidy the garage (once and for all!)	Learn how to fly
Stop procrastinating	Get a new job
Decorate	Stay in a five-star hotel
Be happy	

There must be something in there to get you started.

If you haven't done your list yet and you are reading ahead then can I urge you to stop for a moment and write your list now. Don't ask 'how?' just yet. It's more important to get your list written down.

Then go through each item and do the following:

★ Ask yourself: 'Is this really what I want or was I just in brainstorm mode?'

★ Then ask: 'Is this a short, medium or long-term goal?'

★ Choose five items from each goal category then read the following chapters on how to achieve them.

If you have done the task – and I trust you have (you wouldn't have just kept on reading without doing a life-changing exercise, would you?) – then you have joined a very small percentage of the population who actually know some of what they want and have taken the time to record it.

BRILL BIT

When a plane leaves Singapore for Los Angeles on the world's current longest, non-stop flight, it arrives safely because the pilots know exactly where they are going. Due to high winds and external pressures, they can be flying in the wrong direction (off the flight path) for up to 90% of the time but because they know their final destination they will always get there.

38

SHORT-TERM VISION (THE NEXT 90 DAYS)

My first book is called *How to Be Brilliant* with a strapline of 'Change your ways in 90 days'. I love 90-day plans. They are short enough to create a buzz and excitement but long enough to get results.

I once worked with an area office of a well-known international bank. Out of 86 areas in the UK these guys were rated as 86th. I love taking on jobs like that – there is only one way to go! When I met the new area director (who was invited to 'fix it') he said that he wanted to 'turn things around in the coming year'.

'Let's go for 90 days', I suggested. And with a bit of persuasion, we did. Everyone started with their own 90-day plan, broken down into three 30-day projects with 7-day starts, 14-day middles and 7-day ends. And the results? They went from 86 to number 9, then in the following 90 days to number 6!

You will be amazed at what you can achieve in 90 days

Here are 4 possible areas and suggestions on actions designed to inspire you to take action over the next 90 days. You could make them all happen.

Get fit

It doesn't take years to get fit – it takes 90 days. You could devise a training programme now that will build your stamina, get you motivated and make you feel great. No matter how much of a slob you are, in 90 days you can change.

Have a major clear out

In 90 days you can throw out your rubbish, tidy your wardrobes, decorate, do the garden and sort out your paperwork. The energy you'll create by doing this will spur you on to greater things.

Book, prepare for and go on an adventure

Take a look at your diary, find the date closest to 90 days from now and write the word HOLIDAY or ADVENTURE in big bold letters across each day for a week or so. Visit a high street travel agent (much more exciting than doing it online) and ask them for suggestions to fit your tastes and budget.

Find a new job

It takes around 90 days from commitment to your first day once you have made up your mind to get a new job.

Andy Hampton decided that he would get a new job in the next 90 days and wrote it down. He took massive action and started a proactive search – that means he did more than read the papers. He registered with agencies, told friends what he was doing and called the companies he wanted to work for. Sixty-seven days later he started his new job in a field he loved and (here's the best bit) doubled his salary.

Once you have decided what it's going to be, it's all about the action. Just knowing what you want and that you want to achieve it in the short term is OK but the real secret is to take massive action now to achieve it. What needs to happen in the next 7 days or even the next 24 hours?

BRILL BIT

Short-term vision is made into a reality by taking quick and decisive correct actions – go for it! Massive action = massive results.

39

MEDIUM-TERM VISION (1–5 YEARS)

Where do you see yourself in a few years? Assuming you now know how to get started with your short-term goals, with a little bit of time on your side where do you want to go next?

Think about this for a moment:

★ In 1–5 years you can achieve most major goals. You could find the right person, fall in love, get married, have kids, get divorced and still have a year or two left over.

★ In 1–5 years you could learn a skill, start a company, build your business, sell it and start all over again.

★ In 1–5 years you could find a passion, campaign for change, influence society and make a permanent difference.

★ Or in 1–5 years you could still be doing the same old things, day in day out.

You choose.

It's worth thinking about not only what you want but how committed you are to getting it.

Happy to *read* the books? *Tick*

Happy to *write* a plan? *Tick*

Happy to *do* the hard work? *Ouch!*

When I first started to read books on creating vision and achieving goals I noticed they all had certain common themes. Know what you want, write it down and create a visual image. Then keep the goal close by, looking at it every day. That's all brilliant advice.

The bit that many missed out was the rollercoaster ride of effort, disappointments, joy and setbacks that would happen along the way. I knew setbacks would happen; I'd read hundreds of stories, met dozens of people who all told me the same thing. It was only when it happened that I realised how hard it would be.

Ups and downs

When I set a goal of starting my own company, it was easy. Actually making it happen came out of the blue when I had a serious values clash with my old boss. So, in October 1998 I started my business.

This was going to be easy. One of my best contacts said they would give me two days' work a week to get me started. I was moving back to my home turf and I knew I would be successful.

I wrote my 5-year goals, which included writing a book, creating a two-day course, developing the company name as a well-known brand, presenting to a group of 1000 people, driving a Mercedes and having a successful business with a fantastic team led by my wife and I.

How it actually turned out

Year 1

The company that promised me the two days' work a week let me down; as did *all* the other people who had promised me contracts. I lost my car and was driving a friend's old Subaru with no brakes. Due to a lack of interest I cancelled my first two-day course.

Year 2

My wife left me. I launched my two-day course with seven people in the audience (only three had paid). I couldn't afford to pay myself, never mind a team. Had to change the name of the company due to legal reasons – there goes the brand.

Year 3

Presented to a group of 1200 people and went down a storm – ego on overdrive! Thought, this is it! The phone will be red hot. Six months later – and as a result of speaking to 1200 people – I had picked up NO new work. My ego was well and truly burst. Now 20 people on the two-day course. Get a PA – she saves my life!

Year 4

Started to employ more staff as the business grew. Realised I'd employed too many staff and all the money that was coming in with growth was going out (only twice as fast). Bought my first (used) Mercedes (but couldn't afford to run it!).

Year 5

I was persuaded to join another group of training companies who promised to help me achieve my goal of positively influencing 1,000,000 lives much faster. It was three years before I got out of what turned out to be the worst business deal ever. Still, there was some brilliant news – I began dating my ex-wife.

So, that was the first 5 years of Michael Heppell Ltd. How many times do you think I was tempted to throw in the towel? Guess again, but this time higher.

So, what kept me, and the millions of other people who've had (or have) a 5-year vision, going?

The written goal – even though it wasn't going to my plan I knew in my heart of hearts I was going to get the right outcome. On the way to this right outcome, I now knew I'd had 5 years of training, 5 years of character building and 5 years of ensuring I was equipped for what was going to happen over the next 18 months.

During the next year and a half, I wrote a best-selling book, spoke to groups of 1000 over 30 times, bought a new Mercedes (which I could now afford – just), sold out my 2-day 'How to Be Brilliant' course and, more importantly, remarried Christine – who now runs our business.

Final thoughts

When you create your medium-term vision, build in opportunities to be flexible. Be aware of and be prepared for some serious knocks and remember that persistence in the face of adversity is key to achieving your goals.

BRILL BIT

Five-year goals are challenging. We often overestimate what we can achieve in the short term and underestimate what we can achieve in the long term. Five years sits right on the border.

40

LONG-TERM VISION (5+ YEARS)

Have you a big goal? A life's mission? Something that you would be prepared to spend years, if not decades, working on?

Preparing to play stadiums

Colin Archer and I were both in bands when we were around 17 years old. In fact, most of the 'cool kids' (yes, I was a cool kid) were in a band of some description.

My band, Stage 2, was in the same heat as his band, The Edge, during the North East 'Battle of the Bands' competition. The Edge won and my band came second but there were no hard feelings – they were better than us.

I got to know Colin and even ended up programming a drum machine for him (ironic when you read the rest of this story). One thing that shone out of him was his ability to play guitar. He wasn't just good, he was brilliant.

A few years later, when the dream of pop stardom had passed, I visited Colin in London. He was living in the scruffiest flat I had ever seen. He had nothing, hardly any furniture, very basic essentials and just about the clothes he stood up in. I asked him what he was doing and he said: 'Preparing to play stadiums, Michael.'

Preparing to play stadiums! That wasn't what it looked like to me.

Years went by and we lost touch. I'd often think about him preparing for his stadiums and although he did have some minor success in a couple of bands there were no stadiums yet.

Then in 1999 I heard on the radio that Gem Archer (yep, that's Colin) had been asked by Noel & Liam Gallagher to join Oasis! I can safely say that since then it's been stadiums all the way.

Gem always knew that one day he would achieve his goal. Last year I bumped into him at the port in Ibiza. While we were chatting I asked if he remembered what he said when I asked him what he was doing all those years ago, 'Preparing to play stadiums, Michael'. He had lived with the vision so long it was engrained.

I wonder how many people would have that level of commitment to achieving a long-term goal now. I think I know one – how about YOU!

The dos and don'ts of long-term vision and goals

Do help other people to achieve their goals on the way. Zig Ziglar said: 'If you help enough people to achieve their goals you will achieve yours.'

Don't have a long-term financial goal – I've met loads of people who set a goal to 'be a millionaire'. As soon as they achieve it they think, 'Now what, two million?' Do what you love to do better than anyone else and the million will be a rather nice by-product.

Do have clarity – know what you really want. The more detail you create around your plans, the more you are likely to achieve them.

Don't live in the past – learn from it but don't dwell in it. There are some fantastic lessons to be learned from your past but, remember, the past does not equal the future.

Do build passion – the more passionate you are about your vision, the more energy you will be able to put into it. Plus, as you build your success people will be attracted to helping you along because of your enthusiasm.

Don't listen to those who say you can't, but do listen to all advice. You will meet people (often the ones closest to you) who say you can't do something. Often they are just trying to be protective.

Do break your long-term vision down into short- and medium-term goals. A 20-year vision can start today if you are prepared to take the first actions now. You don't want to be reminiscing in 20 years and saying: 'I wish …'

Don't leave it to chance. Have a strategy and write it down. Without a written strategy you will end up guessing 'what's next' rather than knowing what has to happen and making it so.

Do believe in yourself. Self-doubt is one of the most dangerous enemies of the long-term visionary. Some people call it the 'wedge of doubt' because once a small opening is found the wedge will keep on pushing until the crack appears and grows.

Don't quit. Do you know the story of the drinks inventor who created '4-Up'? It didn't work so he went back to the lab and came up with '5-Up'. Once again, his idea bombed. So, this time he worked hard and created '6-Up'. When this bombed he quit. How do you think he feels now?

Do model other people who have already achieved. If you have a hero who's achieved what you want, study them, meet them, find out how they did it and if you like their method – do the same!

Don't stop learning. The day you think you know it all is the same day you'll start to lose it all. The top earners are the top learners; they never take those 'L' plates off. If you're not achieving your long-term vision ask yourself how much learning you have been participating in to make you an expert in this field?

Do create a visual image to go with your plan (see Chapter 4L).

Having a long-term vision that helps you to jump out of bed on Monday morning with a spring in your step and a smile on your face is the greatest feeling.

BRILL BIT

Make sure your long-term vision represents the core you. That it is in keeping with your values and it contributes to society. If you have a big vision that you feel brilliant about you'll never be stuck for something to do.

WRITTEN PLANS

I've added this section because most people miss it out. I don't know if it's because people don't have the time, don't know how or just can't be bothered. But what I do know is the people who write their plans to accompany their written goals seem to achieve them. Whereas those who don't – don't.

First, the good news. You don't have to write a book. Now the 'could be better' news: you do have to write more than a few words. Finally, some more good news: 90% of all you need is in the next two pages and the rest can be found in other sections of this book.

PPP

Begin by writing your goals using the 3Ps formula. This means ensuring your goals are:

★ **P**ersonal.

★ **P**ositive.

★ **P**resent.

Personal is easy. Just make sure your written goals start with 'I'.

Positive can be more challenging. The important issue here is to ensure you use positive language when you write a goal. If you have a goal to find happiness, then writing 'I no longer want to be sad' uses too many negatives. You will be reading these goals every day, so choose your words carefully.

Present refers to writing your goals in the present tense. In simple terms, writing your goals as if you are already achieving them. For example, if you want to have a brilliant family holiday in Australia write the words: 'I am having a fabulous family holiday in Australia now.' Your brain will want to make sense of this and will create 'Gestalt' (your brain's way of making things have order), which makes you more focused on achieving the goal.

Start planning!

Once you have a list of clearly written goals, it's time to create your plan – and write it down!

Here's an example of the outline of year 1 and year 5 as a written plan for someone who has a 5-year plan to start, build and sell a business.

This is not the business plan; these are the 90-day actions that come together to form a 5-year vision. You will have more details in the early years.

Year 1

1st 90 days	Set up office
	Find a brilliant name
	Protect idea
	Set up bank account, etc.
	Research funding
	Soft launch brand
	Make first sale!
2nd 90 days	Prepare funding presentation
	Secure 12 appointments with funders (one each week)
	Make two more sales
	Recruit operations person (area of weakness)
3rd 90 days	Complete legals with funder
	Make four sales
	Appoint admin assistant
	Develop sales platform
4th 90 days	Create resourcing plan for business
	Go full time
	Attend a Michael Heppell 'Brilliance in Business' course
	End year at breakeven

Year 5

Ensure every system works without me
Have clear exit strategy written
Find buyer
Sell business
Buy yacht

So, what if it doesn't go according to your written plan?

Excellent! At least you know! Without the plan, how would you know if you were going off track? How would you know the right time to move into your new venture full time?

There are so many variables once you start on your journey towards achieving a personal vision. With a written plan you can also document what you will do if these issues arise. Here are seven classics. Write your strategy on how to deal with each of these next to the heading and use these pages as a reference:

1 Lack of support.

2 Running out of time.

3 Not enough resources.

4 Important person says 'no'.

5 Competition.

6 Lack of energy and motivation.

7 Boredom.

Going off track is fine – when you spot it. But what if you don't? What if you don't know there's a wobble? Written plans help you to avoid that. Then you have the opportunity to adjust, refocus and replan.

VISUALISATION

In the year 2000 Muhammad Ali was voted 'Greatest sportsperson of all time'. I can't think of too many people who could claim that crown since, so let's assume he still holds that accolade.

What made him so special?

There are many characteristics that made Ali great (or the greatest) but few were more perfected than his ability to visualise an outcome.

He said that after a press conference he would go back to his hotel room and visualise the preparation for the next fight exactly how he wanted it to be. He would see himself working hard in the gym, pounding the big punch bag and building up stamina. He would imagine what it was like to be back from his early morning run before his opponent had even got out of bed.

Then he would visualise the day of the fight. He'd see the car pulling up outside the venue and he would hear the crowd shouting his name: 'Ali, Ali, Ali.' He would see himself in the changing room and he'd vividly imagine the smells, tastes and noises. He would create the feeling of the bandages being wrapped round his hands and the gloves being tied. Then he would see himself walking to the ring and hear the crowds shouting for him. Once in the ring, he would see his opponent but would make him look small and weak.

Next he would imagine how the fight would be fought. He'd visualise each round right until the moment where he believed he would win and then he would see his opponent fall. After hearing the count and knowing at that moment he had won – he would freeze-frame the image and surround it with brilliant white light.

Future history

That is the image he would visualise when training. That is the image he would see every morning when he woke up and every night when he went to bed. That's the image he would see every time someone mentioned the fight. He called it creating a 'future history'. A future he was so certain of, it was as if the historians had already recorded it.

Is that

For some
and you
to be abl
close you
ideas to h

By no
long-term
The final

Futur

Can you
If so, yo
history r
can to r
magazir

Ther

By doing this on a regular (daily) basis you
focused on achieving your goals and while
for you it does drive you to do it. It keeps
subconscious level and helps to keep

Be careful who you show your fu
they don't share your vision,
they could be pushing it

create a montage of your pictures. You may want to do one for your short-, one for your medium- and one for your long-term vision.

Then, in brightly coloured pen, write the first line of the goal as described in the 'written goals' section and finally write the date when you will have achieved it. Remember to write the date, not just 'three months' or 'one year'.

Now get your future history maps colour copied in various sizes and put them in places where you will see them every day. Stick a small one on your mirror. Put one on your wardrobe door. Laminate an A4 version and study it every night.

Night visualisation

When you look at a goal and read the description, close your eyes and see yourself achieving it. Make it as real as you can, add details, amplify the colour, add taste, smell and feelings. Then when you really feel it is part of you move on to the next image.

become extremely
t doesn't do the work
you focused, works at a
ou on track.

BRILL BIT

ure history maps to. If
as fast as you'll be seeing it coming to you,
way.

43

RESOURCES

Hands up who wants to do all the work themselves, without any help, intervention or resources to make it any easier. Well, that will be ... no one then.

So, how come so many people do just that?

Going solo?

Reinhold Messner was the first person to successfully climb Mount Everest solo (in 1980). Do you know why? Because he's a nutter! Actually, he's widely regarded as the greatest climber of all time, so I thought I would find out more about him. It turns out that when he climbed Everest solo, he had a brilliant team of people helping with the planning, research and setting up for the climb.

So, step one is, even if you a supremely good at something, you still have to surround yourself with the right people.

Next, did he climb Everest in any old climbing gear? No, he had the very best equipment money could buy, some of it specifically designed for this kind of hazardous trip.

Finally, had he just taken up mountaineering? Of course not; he'd been climbing since his childhood. By his early twenties he was regarded as one of Europe's best climbers. By 1970 he was climbing previously unclimbed faces in the Himalayas. And two years before his first solo ascent of Everest, he was the first to climb Everest without oxygen. He was immersed in climbing, he lived and breathed and practised and prepared and pushed his limits.

So, if you're going to achieve your brilliant vision I suggest you take a leaf out of Mr Messner's book and ...

Surround yourself with a brilliant team

If you want to know how successful you are going to be at achieving your goals, take a good look at the five people whom you spend most of your time with. Do they inspire you? Could they achieve the goals you want to achieve?

I have a friend who really wants to quit smoking but she spends most of her spare time with three friends who are smokers. She isn't exactly setting herself up for success with that one, is she?

In order to achieve your vision, start to spend time with people who inspire you. It's amazing to think that you massively increase your chances of success just by spending time with different people.

Terry Laybourne is, in my opinion, one of the best chefs in Britain. When I asked him how he got to be so brilliant, he modestly said: 'Hard work and a bit of luck.' Pressing him further I found that one of the things he did was to continuously surround himself with other brilliant chefs.

When he worked in a five-star hotel in Switzerland he took 'a break' by working in a famous fish restaurant in Newcastle. He wanted to learn from the best. And guess what? He still has that attitude. So, rather than deter other chefs (perhaps competitors), he asks them to 'guest' in his kitchen at a special night or as part of an annual food festival.

By finding the right people to spend time with you will raise your game. You'll be surprised at how much that will help you.

But what if you believe they don't want to lend a hand? You need to use these magic words: 'I need your help.' I believe there is an inbuilt programme in most people that clicks into gear when they hear those words. Test it – you'll love the results as people do whatever they can to help you.

Get the right kit

What equipment do you need? Go for the best you can afford. If you need a computer get a fast, reliable one. If you need internet access go for the fastest you can afford. If you need some specialist items to do what you need to do, then invest in them.

If you have to write, use a good pen and record your actions in a journal. Finally, if you need to get something designed, get a designer to do it. It saves time and looks so much better.

Knowledge is king

Ultimately, get the best knowledge. We have never lived in better times for having abundant knowledge around us. The biggest challenge we have these days is too much information.

So, make a commitment to seeking out the knowledge that you need and make the most of every learning opportunity, whether formal or informal. Here's how to get the best out of some of the key methods of learning.

Classroom

Sit as close to the front and centre as you can. Commit to turning up for every session. Get there early. Take lots of notes. Ask questions – especially the daft ones that everyone else was thinking but only you would dare to ask. Reread your notes immediately after the class and before the next one. Do homework on the day you get it.

Reading

Mentally rehearse reading before you do it. Read with a highlighter pen and good-quality blue or red pen. Highlight the bits that jump out or need further clarification. Make notes in the margin. Write to the author.

Did you know that if you read 100 books on a specialist subject and digested the information, you could become one of the top 10 experts in the world in that field?

Coaching

Be open; it's not your job to know all the answers. Ask for advice and don't be intimidated by a coach who says, 'How would you do it?' when you ask them a question. Take lots of notes. Replay what you have learned to check you understood it.

Audio

A fantastic way to learn, but your mind will wander. Again, take notes. Be prepared to listen to each CD or download several times. Find a picture of the person presenting the programme and visualise them speaking. If you can't get a picture, create in your mind a picture of your best ever trainer and see them presenting the audio.

Observation

Be like the meerkat and keep your head up. Notice what people are doing. Study the causes and effects. Ask people questions. Listen carefully to the answers.

Video, DVD and TV

Watch at a desk. Schedule how much time is needed. Imagine you are there with the presenter. Find the pause and rewind buttons and use them. Watch in a small group and discuss the outcomes.

Learning, and becoming an expert, is a surefire way to help you achieve your goals. The knowledge you gain will propel you at ever higher speeds and enable you to achieve your goals more effectively.

When you have the right resources, you will feel more comfortable about starting your journey. You may have to pick some more up on the way but it's vital to ensure you have what you need around you to make your vision a reality.

BRILL BIT

Beware of learning a lot then not doing anything with it.
Many 'experts' end up with masses of knowledge they just forget to do anything practical with.

PART SEVEN
YOUR CAREER

44

THE CAREER
WHEEL

It's one of the biggest areas in your life. Most people spend a third of their lives at work, so take a long, hard, honest look at how well you are doing.

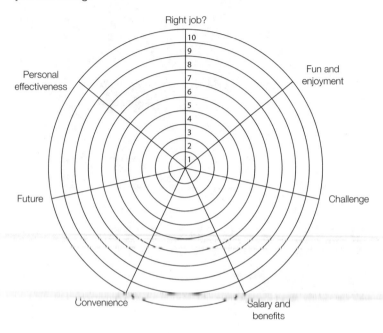

Right job?

Are you doing the job of your dreams or is it a nightmare? Perhaps you started with a brilliant job and things have changed. If you know you are in the right job then give yourself a high mark. If you are not sure if this is the right job (or think maybe you've changed and your job hasn't) then you may be midway. Or if you're an 'I can't stand it!' then I'm presuming you'll give yourself a low, low mark on this spoke.

Fun and enjoyment

Do you enjoy your work? Is it a fun place to be with lots of smiles or is it a place of negativity? How much do you contribute to the current climate? Give yourself a mark for how much fun and enjoyment you're having at work.

Challenge

Are you challenged, tested, given an opportunity to grow and be better? Or do you feel like you are functioning at less than 50% of your ability? If you are enjoying the challenge and being persuaded to increase your role then it's a high mark. If you are bored out of your tiny skull then you can give yourself a 2. Or you may land somewhere in between.

Salary and benefits

Are you earning too much money? Are there too many perks in your job for you to handle? Then, lucky you – you're a 12 out of 10! There aren't too many of you, so if you are happy with your salary and benefits you'll get a high mark. If you'd like a little more and feel undervalued then you'll lose a couple of marks here. And if you think 'I need to double my salary and fast' then give yourself a low mark and jump to Chapter 48 on salary and benefits to find out how.

Convenience

Does your work fit your lifestyle or does your lifestyle have to fit around your work? Is your daily commute driving you crazy or is it the lousy working hours that are getting you down? That all adds up to a low score. Or you may have a wonderful journey to work and hours that suit your needs. If that's you, it's good news – and high marks.

Future

How does your future career look? If you're stuck in a rut, then what are you doing about it? Is it time to find a new career? Or are you delighted with your working future, knowing it will bring you fulfillment for years to come? Give yourself a mark for how you view your career in the future.

Personal effectiveness

How good are you at what you do? Are you a leading light or just 'part of the team'? If you want to get better at what you do, but you're just not sure how, then here's an opportunity for you to give yourself an honest mark. If you need a little help then turn to Chapter 51 on personal effectiveness and find out how to shine.

All done? Good, join up your scores and take a look at your Career Wheel. Do you need some help? You're in good company: 80% of people are dissatisfied in some way with their careers. Read on to find out how to join the top 20% who love theirs!

45

RIGHT JOB?

The question you need to ask yourself about your current job is simply: 'Is this really what I want to do?' If the answer is 'no', then stage one is not to beat yourself up over it as the chances are that when you took the job there was a very good reason for it. It's just that things change.

So, decision time: do you want to improve what you have right now or find a new job? I'll help you deal with both options.

Let's start with improving what you have right now. When you started in your chosen job there must have been some compelling reasons why you chose it as a career. Let's see what type of person you are.

Give yourself a score out of 10 for the following:

		Least like me							Most like me		
		1	2	3	4	5	6	7	8	9	10
a	I'd like more money										
b	I'd like something more interesting										
c	I'd like a greater challenge										
d	I'd like to be promoted										
e	I'd like to work less										
f	I'd like an easy working life for lots of money										

Now rate these:

	1	2	3	4	5	6	7	8	9	10
1 I'm happy to work harder										
2 I'm creative and resourceful										
3 I ask for more to do										
4 I like responsibility										
5 I'm prepared to be paid less										
6 I believe in fairies										

If you gave yourself high marks for a, b, c and d then you'll have to be prepared to have high marks for 1, 2, 3 and 4. If you gave a high mark for e, then the chances are high you'll have to accept 5 and if you have a high mark for f then you MUST have a high mark for 6.

Breathe life into your current job

It is common for jobs to change greatly in a short time. Responsibilities change, bosses change, targets change. The job you're doing today may not be the one you applied for and you didn't see it coming. So, what can you do about it? You can start by looking at what you want from the lists and asking if you are prepared to do what is necessary to achieve them.

Look back at the core reason why you took this career path. I often work with teachers, some of whom complain about how terrible their working lives are. During my keynote presentations, I'll challenge the audience with: 'If you don't love it – don't do it.'

For teachers, I add: 'Remember what you do for a living. You are directly involved with improving the quality of life for often some of the most vulnerable people in our society. You have the best job in the world!'

Teachers can get caught up in politics, legislation, funding, working conditions and a million other issues. I like to remind them of what attracted them to teaching in the first place.

Remind yourself of the core reasons why you wanted your current job.

Next, rewrite your job description. This preparation is a vital part of the process. Write the type of job you want to do within your organisation. Next, if you are a valuable member of the organisation, ask for a review with your boss. If you feel you aren't a valuable member of your team then meet your boss and have a discussion about that first.

This next stage only works if you are a cherished component of the organisation. Tell them how you are feeling and present them with your new job description. Ask how close you can get to that description in the next 90 days. If you are a valued member of the team I'll guarantee you'll get most of what you ask for.

Now, with your re-energised belief in what you are doing, throw yourself into your brilliant job. And if it doesn't work out you can always ...

Find a new job

It may be that you have just reached the end of your time with your current job and it's time to move on. Read Chapter 50; you'll get the motivation and the plan to go out there and find the job you really want.

How to leave your job brilliantly

Martin Beeson worked for me as a marketing manager; he's very bright and came from a corporate giant to our considerably smaller business. Six months into his appointment, he asked for a meeting and told me that he wanted to get back into the world of large-scale marketing. Although working with a small team was fun, he didn't see a long-term future with me. He wanted me to know that he would be looking for jobs and would I be a referee.

Two weeks later he showed me three jobs he was interested in and asked for my opinion. A few days later he asked me to look over his application and give him some thoughts and advice.

A week later he asked to book a day's holiday to go for an interview. He got the job. Martin then worked three weeks' notice and moved to London to work for BMI. What a perfect way to leave.

Here's how not to do it!

Have a look of guilt when your boss sees you reading the jobs section in your paper. Use company time to apply for a job. Lie to your boss saying you have a doctor's appointment when you really have an interview. Tell your workmates before you tell your boss that you've been offered a new position.

I have a brilliant relationship with Martin; we have stayed friends and I was happy to be a referee when he applied for his visa to move to Australia. He stays in touch, I'd give him a reference any day and I'm proud to say I know him.

Then there are other people who have worked for me who … well, let's not go there.

Be proactive

What do you really love to do? What gives you energy rather than taking it away? Write a list of everything you love to do then see if you can build a career around that.

Don't wait for your dream job to be advertised in the newspaper. Register with agencies, find the type of organisation you want to work for and try to meet with senior people from that organisation. Ask them what they are looking for in new staff and ask them when they will next be recruiting.

Final thought

How do you know you're in the right job or career? Easy, the same way you know when you're not. You feel it!

BRILL BIT

Every time you complain about your work, your bosses or how bad things are, you are demonstrating and reaffirming your lack of courage to do something about it. If you think you are being unfulfilled, lack challenge, respect and value, it's worth taking a look in the mirror and exploring the likely source.

FUN AND ENJOYMENT

Work and fun should go together like fish and chips. But often the only time they end up in the same sentence is when disgruntled employees say: 'Work is no fun.'

So, can it be and should it be? Some people would say it depends on your job. Not true. I've met many people who, on the face of it, have the most serious jobs in the world: undertakers, tax inspectors and the like, who have loads of fun at work. I've also met nursery workers, clowns and comedians (yes, comedians) who are truly miserable.

What makes work dull?

The most common cause of a dreary day comes from lack of variety. Although having said that, when I was 16 I visited the United Biscuits factory and saw how they made Jaffa Cakes. The process was amazing but perhaps the most amazing part was meeting Doris, who, with the aid of a long stick with a spike in it, removed the Jaffa Cakes that weren't up to scratch. Imagine looking at a constant stream of Jaffa Cakes 10 wide for 8 hours a day seeking out the ones with dodgy sponge or wobbly chocolate. For the other two units they changed the person doing that job every 60 minutes but on Doris's shift only she had that role. The human resources manager took us to one side and announced that Doris had done the same job for 30 years. There was a gasp from our group and feeling that it must be terrible. Even then my brain worked differently from the rest of the crowd and I spotted something that most people didn't. SHE LOVED IT! Doris was the only person who had a smile on her face, she sang with the radio, chatted with her friends and took great pride in her work. *And* she gave us all a dodgy Jaffa Cake!

What's the secret?

There are several factors that come into play when you are deciding whether work should be fun. And that was the first one – did you spot it? 'Deciding' that work should be fun. Step one is about making that all-important decision: 'Do I want to have fun at work?'

The obvious answer is 'yes', but I believe that's a misconception. Some people choose not to have fun at work because it's easier for them to be negative and by being negative they get more significance.

Here's a scenario: five work mates go out for lunch; very quickly the conversation turns to the 'nightmare of a day' that one of them is having. Have you ever overheard a conversation that goes something like this?

FIRST MATE   *'I'm having a nightmare today, everything's going wrong. The server has gone down and we haven't had email for two hours, I don't know how I'm going to get through all of my work.'*

SECOND MATE   *'That's nothing, at least your boss likes you; mine has had it in for me all week. I'm sure she wants me out.'*

THIRD MATE   *'You think that's bad. We're right in the middle of a major restructure and everyone is being given even more responsibility. I think this is the final straw.'*

Now, just imagine if a fourth person jumped in with:

FOURTH MATE   *'I'm having a brilliant week. This morning we had such a laugh in the weekly meeting and on Friday it's my turn to bring in biscuits. I thought I'd make monster gingerbread men.'*

How do you think the rest of the people at the table would react? Do you think they would:

★ Say how nice it was to hear someone was having so much enjoyment at work and ask for advice on how to make their workplace more fun?

★ Complain that, 'It's alright for some', before continuing the 'why my life's worse than yours' competition?

★ Wish their work life was as much fun, but hate the thought of actually doing anything about it as they get much more attention being negative?

The challenge is we often do get more attention for being negative and miserable than for being positive and having fun. So, are you ready to break the mould?

Could you be the first Minister of Fun for your department or organisation?

Here are some simple things you can do to make work lighter and more enjoyable:

★ Organise **a standing ovation.** If you have a hero at work, arrange with your buddies to give them a standing round of applause. It's a hoot and I've yet to meet the person who's getting too much recognition.

★ **Celebrate 'hireversaries'.** Have a celebration for the dates when people started working with you.

★ **Spice up your voicemail.** 'I'm either on the phone or away from my desk' is the most boring message in the world. Why not: 'Sorry I can't pick up in person. I'm currently on a top secret mission to make internal auditing fun again – I may be gone for some time … only kidding. I'm in all day so leave a message.'

★ **The power of plants!** Fill your office or working area with plants and flowers. It makes you smile, your colleagues smile and the planet smile too.

★ **Dress-up Wednesday.** Everyone does dress-down Friday; why not dress up on a Wednesday?

★ **Create an alias.** Invent an evil nickname for the unpleasant side of your personality and when you feel yourself being negative just say: 'That wasn't me, it was Wicked Wendy, Dreadful Dave, etc…'

★ **Complain to yourself.** If you want to have a moan, leave a message on your own voicemail or send yourself an email. Once you've listened to it or read it, if you still think others need to hear it then go ahead.

★ **Have a backward meeting.** That means you start with the date of the next meeting and work back to apologies.

★ **LAUGH!!!** Find an opportunity to laugh every day. Laugh at your mistakes. Laugh at yourself. Laugh with each other.

If after testing these ideas for 90 days, you still feel like you're working in 'negatyville', then perhaps it's time for you to find a workplace where you can have some fun.

BRILL BIT

Give the office equipment names. *Everyone* should have a printer called Brian.

47

CHALLENGE

Everyone loves a challenge. Well, they do if they feel they can meet that challenge. The bigger crisis comes when you don't feel equipped with the right skills to tackle the challenge.

Hungarian-born Mihaly Csikszentmihalyi has a theory that, if you get two key measures – the levels of challenge and skill – functioning at a high level, you will work in a place called 'flow'. He describes 'flow' as: 'Being completely involved in an activity for its own sake. The ego falls away. Time flies. Every action, movement, and thought follows inevitably from the previous one ... Your whole being is involved, and you're using your skills to the utmost.'

Does that sound like you at work?

Here's how to show Csikszentmihalyi's theory of 'flow' in diagrammatic form.

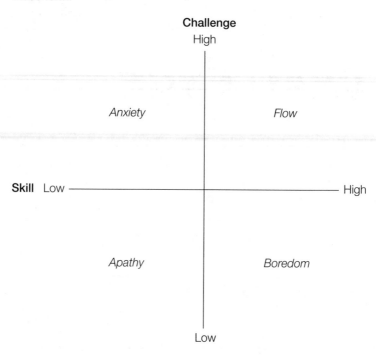

In simple terms, if you have a low challenge and low skills to deal with it, then apathy sets in. If you have a high challenge and low skills, then anxiety prevails (remember your first driving lesson?).

If you have a low challenge and high skill, then obviously you are going to be bored. The magic quadrant is when you have a high challenge and you also have the high skills – that's flow!

Flow can often be seen in sports. Tennis players talk of how the game seemed to be slow motion or athletes talk about being 'in the zone'. Can the same be said for your work?

I believe so. Have you had a time when you were working on a project or had a special task to complete? The hours would fly by because you enjoyed and were totally engaged in what you were doing. Remember that strong sense that you were achieving something? Then you were in flow.

Would you like to experience that again?

Here are some of the key ingredients to get into flow:

★ Have a clearly defined goal. It's almost impossible to get into flow unless you know your outcomes. When a tennis player is in flow it's because they know they have to win.

★ Create an environment for flow. Without the right resources available and a 'stop-start' working day you will experience more frustration than flow.

★ Support from your 'sponsor'. This may be your manager, a colleague, customer or other party who is reliant on the results. If you aren't getting support from these people be proactive and ask them for clear direction and time to discuss your project.

There are some other benefits to flow too. Jim Clifton, CEO of the Gallup Organization, says: 'People with high flow never miss a day. They never get sick. They never wreck their cars. Their lives just work better.'

Asking for a bigger challenge

One of the main reasons why you won't have felt challenged is because your boss thinks you are working at your limit. I'm not sure where they pick that up from, but they will continue to think that until you change their thinking. If you want a bigger challenge, don't wait for them to give it to you – ask!

A note for the self-employed

Remember when you first started your business, you were bright eyed and ready for anything. Then once you 'got on top' of things you felt like you were in a comfortable place and you could start to relax. Then your business became a routine.

Here's a question for you. If you scored low on your level of challenge and you own a business, what would you need to do to double the size of your organisation in the next 12 months? Do you feel challenged now?

Growth = challenge. Staying still effectively means you are going backwards, you'll lose interest, your staff may get bored and you'll inadvertently put your business at risk. Go for growth and feel the flow!

BRILL BIT

'Please, sir, can I have some more?'

When little Oliver Twist asked for some more, he was given a thrashing; when you ask for some more (a greater challenge), you'll be a hero. Think about it: if you were the boss and a member of your team asked you for a greater challenge how would you feel?

48

SALARY AND BENEFITS

want more! The easiest way to earn more money is to add more value first – then ask for the pay rise. Unfortunately, most of the people who complain about not earning enough have an attitude of: 'When I get paid more *then* I'll do more.'

Right now you are getting paid exactly what you are worth. If you disagree then look at it like this:

★ Have you added significantly more value in the eyes of the person who pays you?

★ If you aren't getting paid enough, have you asked for more?

★ Have you been prepared to move jobs and been successful in finding a new job with the salary you require?

If you have answered 'no' to one or more of these questions, then whose fault is it that you aren't, in your opinion, 'being paid what you are worth'?

My job isn't to beat you up – it's to wake you up. Understand the main reasons why you may not be getting paid more, then if you want more follow this plan.

I do appreciate that this approach is more difficult in larger companies or organisations who have rigid pay scales and structure. However, I have yet to meet the person who hasn't increased their pay, benefits or both by using this system.

★ *Add more value first*. I know I keep on writing this but that's because it is the most important step towards increasing your salary. Adding value means doing more than is being asked or expected. Show up early, smash your targets, have solutions to problems before they take over, be brilliant for your customers. You get the idea. It should feel hard.

★ *Think like your boss* (or the person who decides on salaries). Why should they give you more? If they have a set budget and they have the unenviable task of sharing it between you and the other people you work with, why should you get a bigger slice of the pie?

★ *Make a list* of important accomplishments you have achieved in the past three months. You may want to go back further but the more current the better.

★ *Add to profit.* In business, profit is king. In the public sector, adding more value is king. If you can add to the bottom line and increase profitability via improved income or reduced costs, then do it. This could be the money your boss is looking for to pay your increase in salary.

★ *Get your timing right.* Applying for promotion or a salary increase too soon can set you back.

★ *Focus on projects that add the maximum value.* You don't get a pay rise by saying yes to everything – you get tired.

OK, so you're prepared to ask for more money. Did I mention you'll have to ask? There aren't too many organisations that will request to meet with you and then offer you a bumper pay rise (and I'm not talking about your annual pay increase).

So how do you ask?

Here are five potential questions you may have and thoughts for the answers.

1 When is the best time to ask for a pay rise?

The good times to ask are:

★ during reviews

★ when your organisation is being successful

★ when you have been given additional responsibility

★ at the end of a day (fewer distractions).

The bad times are:

★ after a full pay review (why didn't you ask then?)

★ following redundancies

★ when your organisation is struggling (unless you are their only hope!)

★ informally ('excuse me boss, have you got a minute?').

2 What is the best way to approach your boss?

Ask for a face-to-face meeting (if they have a PA, book it through them) and tell them you want to discuss your future. At this point, if you are a valuable member of staff your boss may be feeling slightly sick.

They will want to organise a meeting as soon as possible. Don't take the meeting there and then, even if they say: 'Well, now is a good time.' Now isn't necessarily the best time for you.

3 What should you do to prepare?

Have written evidence of what you have achieved and why this will make a difference to your organisation. Find out what you can about similar salaries for comparable jobs. If you feel underpaid have a copy of these salaries for your meeting.

Prepare yourself, think about this like another interview (only this time they know you) and make sure you look like you're worth the extra money.

Have in mind what you will be happy to accept and what you will do if you don't get what you ask for (or close to it).

4 What else should be on the table?

Keep the whole package in mind. Plan carefully what you want. Suddenly throwing in 'And can I have a couple of extra days' holiday', without thinking it through, makes you look desperate and weakens your position. Stick to the type of benefits your organisation normally offers.

5 What affects salary negotiation?

★ Does your boss like you? I know this shouldn't be on the agenda and they should only be looking at you from a professional point of view, but your likeability factor is going to play a big part. Your likeability is based on how you fit with their values system so it's worth knowing what they are.

★ Cash flow, especially for smaller businesses and budgeting for bigger organisations.

★ Your significance to the organisation – measured like this. First – at that moment. Second – in the future. Third – in the past.

★ Your reputation. If you have a reputation for jumping from one job to another to build your career, a smart boss won't pay more to try to keep you as they'll know you'll move on soon anyway. You're better off having a reputation for successes and hard work.

Three final thoughts

1 Don't pretend you have been offered another job if you haven't – you'll get found out.

2 Do your homework in your own time and subtly let your boss know that you did it at home.

3 Add even more value when you do get your pay rise. Let the decision maker know they made a good decision.

BRILL BIT

Remember that everyone is dispensable, but some are less so than others. Your level of dispensability will be the number one factor in your salary negotiations.

CONVENIENCE

Do you fit round work or does work fit round you? Many years ago some companies started to introduce a brilliant system called 'flexitime'. Flexitime meant you could clock in and clock out when you wanted so long as you covered your core working week. You could even store up hours and take extra days off. Some other companies have a version of flexitime called 'max-your-time' (made-up name), which usually means you work all the hours God sends and don't take *any* time off. Where flexitime left offices empty on a Friday afternoon with most staff choosing to do an extra hour here and there so they could take a long weekend, 'max-your-time' workers could be seen ordering pizzas at 10 pm and seriously contemplating bringing a sleeping bag to work. There has to be another way.

Your hours

What if you wanted to finish work at 3 pm so you could pick the kids up from school? What if you wanted every other Friday off? What if you could take an extended lunch on Tuesdays and Thursdays to play tennis? I know people who have full-time jobs who were able to negotiate all of those scenarios, because they knew the most important rule in time negotiation: give to get.

It's so much easier to negotiate some flexibility in your working hours if you're not a 'clock watcher'. Give a few hours first, then when it feels like you have enough deposits in your boss's 'emotional bank account' ask for the trade-off. All the people in those examples did that by (in order): getting in really early; working until 6 pm instead of 5; and only taking 15 minutes for lunch on Mondays, Wednesdays and Fridays.

The trade-off

Life is often about choices. It can be challenging to have a career that involves lots of travelling when you have children. With this in mind there will always be times when you need to trade off the pros and cons for the greater good. A good way to think about it is to ask the classic question, 'How will I feel about this in 5 or 10 years from now?' There are few people who will say they're glad they missed the school play because they were finishing that flippin' monthly report.

Convenient?

I live nine minutes from my office; it's a five-mile country drive to the nearest major road then only four minutes along a speedy dual carriageway to our office. Today I decided not to go to the office; instead I went for a long walk, had some lunch and now I'm in my study typing this book while occasionally looking into my garden. At the moment, I'd like to give myself a 10 for convenience.

Last Wednesday I woke at 4.15 am, rushed to get a taxi to the airport, checked in, joined the longest security queue of all time, got on my plane, sat next to the world snoring champion, got off the plane and on to a train. Then into another taxi before arriving at a meeting which lasted for 45 minutes. Then I took a train, a taxi and a walk to another meeting, before heading back to the airport to join the second longest security queue. Only to sit on a plane with a wonderful three-year-old who looked like he was going to be sick for most of the flight, then back into another taxi and home by 9 pm. On that day, the convenience of my working day would be around … 2?

I'm lucky; I have very few days like that but I know people who have that kind of aggravation every day. They have to do the work, but it is very inconvenient to do so.

Lemmings

Over a million people in the UK have a commute to their work that takes them more than an hour. Ouch!

Well, you could move closer to where you work? No? OK, I get it, house prices, short-term plans, the wrong schools, etc. You *must* commute. So let's make the most of it.

How do you turn this wasted time into priceless pleasure? First question: 'Are you driving or have you delegated that to someone else like the train driver?' Obviously, if you are driving to work each day, you can't read (no, really, you can't – even in traffic jams!) but there are other things you can do to make your journey fly by.

Here are seven ways to get the most out of your commute

1 Listen to audio programmes – which make you better!

I know the radio is easy, but is it making you a better person or is it just background chatter?

There are loads of brilliant audio programmes on masses of subjects from leadership to loving. Check out **www.audible.co.uk** (or **.com**) for thousands of titles on just about everything. If you start now and listen to one title every week you'll be an expert in just six months. Then you can find a job closer to home and get a pay rise!

2 Be a radio guest

Here's a fun game to play if you listen to radio shows that have guests. When the interviewer asks them a question, turn down the volume and answer that question. Quite amusing and works best if you say your answers out loud.

3 Drivers – save the planet!

I have a friend who passed the time on his drive home by wanting to break his record (52 mins during term time). It was unlikely that he would do this as his journey normally takes around an hour. So now he plays a different game called 'save the planet'. Before he leaves for his commute he resets his car's dashboard computer and aims to beat his average 'mpg' for the journey. He's as competitive with himself as ever but to win he has to drive more economically.

4 Start a conversation, if you dare!

I love the tube. I start conversations with strangers and because I don't live in the capital I've never been taught the number one rule of using public transport in London, which seems to be: 'Never ever talk to anyone.' I can't be blamed for my 'overfriendly' behaviour, it's who I am.

So here's a challenge for you. What if you were, you know, to talk to someone – there, I said it! First of all, what's the worst that can happen? No, you won't get beaten up; the worst is they won't talk back. But what if they do? What if you meet a really interesting person? It takes a bit of practice to start conversations with strangers but stick in, it's worth it. Here's a tip. It's easier to start conversations with people on the way home, especially on Fridays, first.

5 Read something you normally wouldn't

We tend to read the same old things and by doing so you associate your commute with this type of reading. Break your pattern and read something that is completely outside your sphere.

6 Sharpen your mind

There are more ways to improve your mental agility than doing Sudoku. By spending 30 minutes a day on puzzles you'll improve your brain power and waken your mind before a new day.

7 Knit for the needy

Liz knits two hats and four mittens every week during her train journeys. She sends them to Samaritans Purse who distribute them to children who will be feeling the cold this winter.

> **BRILL BIT**
>
> If you find it difficult to fit in time to exercise, see how many simple exercises you can do while commuting. From simple breathing routines to the famous butt clench, you'll be amazed at what you can do.

FUTURE

There has been a lot of information in this section about making the most of your career right now – but what about your future? What if you do have to move on and get a new job? What if you need to find a totally new career? When is too late *really* too late and how do you go about getting your dream job?

Imagine yourself …

Add 10 years on to your age. Can you see yourself doing what you do now in 10 years' time when you're ____? If you can that's brilliant or you may just need a little tweak to make your future career perfect. But what if that concept scared you silly? What if you need a serious rethink about your working future? Well, now must be as good a time as any. It's time to get your head out of the sand and realise there are thousands of brilliant careers out there; many are designed perfectly for you and the people who are recruiting need people with your skills. I often hear people say they stick with their current job 'because it's safe'. Trust me, no job is safe. What an awful way to live a third of your life, not really loving what you do, just because it seems to be safe.

Going to work should be one of the most exciting parts of your life, not just something you do to pay the bills. The rest of this chapter is going to get you focused on finding the best career for you.

What's your perfect future?

First, take a moment to follow these simple steps to get the excitement back.

Answer these three questions honestly:

1 If you could do any job with your current skills and knew you would be successful, what would it be?

2 If you could work anywhere in the world, where would it be?

3 If you could write your own pay cheque and were prepared to do whatever it takes to get it, how much would it be?

If you're looking at a piece of paper which says 'Flipping burgers in Stoke for 50 quid a week', then I don't think you've quite grasped the concept. I asked 10 people to do this exercise today and here are my favourite three to inspire you:

> In 10 years I'll be running my own company advising small retailers how to maximise their businesses. I'll get home to my family at night and I'll earn over £100,000.

> In 10 years I'll be the boss here. I love it. I just want his job; he must make at least £30k!

> In 10 years' time I will be working in Formula 1, travelling the world and earning … who cares what I'll earn, I'll be working in Formula 1!

Now do yours before moving on.

Take action

So, now you've done the exercise, how do you create the future career you dreamed of? Well, you can start by ticking everything off this list:

★ I have met someone who is doing that job and asked them for advice.
★ I know the qualifications/experience I need and where to get them.
★ I am prepared to work for 10 years on achieving this goal.
★ I am happy to move out of my comfort zone and take some risks.
★ I have a written plan on how I am going to achieve it.

What if you can tick the list, but you still aren't in the right job now?

Here's how to get a brilliant new job in half the time

Make sure your CV is up to date and tailored for the job you are going for. Ensure covering letters are specific.

I asked some professional recruiters for advice on what they like and don't like on CVs and covering letters. Here's what they said:

'Tell me what you've done. Job titles and company names mean little compared with what you have achieved.'

'List your last job first, please.'

'Only give one email address. When I get CVs with two, I think, can't they organise themselves enough to just have one email address?'

'Use nice paper. 80gm paper feels like tissue paper compared with 100 or 120.'

'Let me think you have produced this CV just for me. Even if you are applying for 50 jobs, personalise it a little and make me think you have written it for me.'

'Everyone writes "Enjoy reading and socialising with friends". What do you read and what does socialising mean? I want to know a little more about you.'

'If I get a letter which starts Dear Sir/Madam it goes straight in the bin. My name is on the advert – use it!'

'Intrigue me, make me want to meet you.'

'Search for yourself on the internet. Remember *what you can see, I can see*, so unless you're really proud of your weekend in Magalut and the pictures posted of you with your mates, then start deleting.'

There's no such thing as an 'I only' job

It's worthwhile doing a skills audit and really considering what you are good at and how those skills can be transferred into other situations. There are no 'I only' jobs:

★ 'I only work in a shop.' Actually you deal with the public (and all their foibles), you manage stock, you are responsible for money, you are able to work different shifts, you understand the essence of great customer service.

★ 'I do administration.' Actually you are a completer/finisher, you support a team of six people, you develop new systems to support the organisation, you're organised and reliable.

I'm sure you get the idea. The skills you have learned are very valuable – from this moment on you never 'only do' anything!

Interviews

So, your application was brilliant and you've got to the next stage – the interview.

Get it in context

I once interviewed for a new personal assistant and we had a shortlist of six people. My first question was: 'Tell me a little bit about yourself.' We had many different replies, some who took us through their working careers from leaving school, others who focused on their technical strengths and one who said: 'Well, I'm a left-handed Sagittarian who can do tarot cards.' Brilliant answer – if she was applying for a game show.

Get tested

Interviewers will often try to catch you out so be prepared by asking some people with interviewing experience to test you. Even if you don't get the questions you rehearse you'll still increase your confidence.

Blend in

Dress smart but neutral and don't wear aftershave or perfume. Introduce them to your multi-coloured socks, bright ties, outrageous jewellery and vintage shoes after you've got the job.

You'll be familiar with everything else, about being enthusiastic, having a firm handshake and telling the truth, etc., but will you do it? Remember, the secret isn't in the knowing, it's in the doing.

Your 10-year career future starts here.

BRILL BIT

If you really want a job, offer to work for the organisation for free for 90 days to prove your value. Make the agreement that at the end of that period if you have impressed they will agree to give you a full-time job and to pay you what you are worth.

51

PERSONAL EFFECTIVENESS

et's assume you *do* want to stay in your current job. You do enjoy what you do and you are happy with your salary (for now). How do you like the idea of being one of the best in the world at what you do?

Here's a set of simple questions that will form the foundation of your own personal effectiveness. Decide how many of the following 10 statements apply to you:

1   I get on well with people and quickly build rapport.

2   I am flexible in my team role.

3   I know how to ask the right questions to get the knowledge I require.

4   I am able to influence others to gain their support.

5   I am seen as a positive person.

6   I am well organised.

7   I am able to manage my time effectively.

8   I feel able to articulate my point of view to anyone.

9   I have a wide range of problem-solving techniques.

10 I am able to manage myself.

If you have scored eight or more then you have the foundations in place to be personally effective in your career. But what if you have fewer? Here are the five key areas to focus on:

1   *Attitude.* Your mental attitude, including belief in yourself and positive approach, will have the biggest single bearing on your personal effectiveness. Every other area will be magnified or minimised because of your attitude.

2   *Organisational skills.* It's very difficult to be personally effective if you are working in chaos. Having orderly working practices, a brilliant filing system and a well-managed working day are essential to achieving this goal.

3   *People skills.* You can't do it all on your own, so your ability to influence other people is one of the most important tools in your effectiveness box.

4 *Creativity*. Your ability to solve problems and find a better way will add to your value much more than hard work alone. Ideas are a currency, so find ways to create as many high-value ones as you can.

5 *Communication skills*. You can have the best ideas and be the most organised, effective person in your team, but unless you can communicate those ideas to others successfully you'll struggle to be all you can be.

With those five keys and scoring eight plus in the personal effectiveness test, you are ready to go to the next step.

Brilliance benchmarking

To be personally effective at the highest level you need to aim for and produce results higher than you ever thought possible. I call the process 'brilliance benchmarking'.

In my book *How to Be Brilliant*, I claimed that if you did a 'good' job you would end up getting 'poor' results. At the time I had people contact me to tell me that they thought this was demotivating. And it can be, if you stop at that point – it's even demotivating at the next level where you only get 'good' results for doing a 'fantastic' job. However, there is one more level and it's attained by pushing beyond fantastic and giving a little more than you ever believed you could. That level is brilliance. And here's the exciting part – when you do a brilliant job you get ... brilliant results!

This is the level where your personal effectiveness is working at its highest point.

So, how do you get to brilliance as your benchmark when it comes to personal effectiveness?

★ *Model others – who already have it*. If you work with or know someone who is brilliant in your chosen area then model what they do. Find out as much as you can about the way they operate. Study their thinking processes and beliefs, then model those traits as closely as you can.

★ *Use CANI.* **C**ontinuous **A**nd **N**everending **I**mprovement. Be your best critic. Ask yourself: 'How could I make this even better?' Study the Japanese principle of *kaizen*, which was made famous by the Toyota production system.

★ *Think transferable.* How can you take the best ways of working from other sectors and apply them to your vocation? What can you learn from sports? How can you transfer ideas from the world of entertainment? What is there in the best manufacturing processes that can help you? Can you learn something from the healthcare sector? Look beyond your field and use your brilliant creativity to transfer ideas to make you even better.

★ *Be in competition – with yourself.* Michael Jordan was arguably the world's greatest basketball player. When he was still on the practice court, long after his team mates had left, his coach asked him: 'Who do you still have to beat?' Michael Jordan replied: 'Me.'

★ *Take massive action.* Remember? Massive action = Massive results. By increasing your pace and taking massive (correct) action, you will get to brilliance faster and enjoy the benefits for longer.

BRILL BIT

If you could create a new job title for yourself, one that really summed up the person you ultimately wanted to become in your career, what would it be? Chief Executive and Managing Director are dull titles. Could you be the first 'Head of global WOW' or 'Chief influencing officer'? Go crazy and I dare you, no, double dare you, to get it put on to a brass plaque ready to go on your door.

PART EIGHT
YOUR PERSONAL
DEVELOPMENT

52

THE PERSONAL DEVELOPMENT WHEEL

A lthough this is the last wheel in the book it is, perhaps, the most important. Your personal development links with every other wheel, so it's critical you get a balance in this area. So let's begin by completing your Personal Development Wheel now.

Positive attitude

How positive are you? Is the glass half-full or half-empty? If problems emerge do you choose to look at them in a positive way or do you feel negativity creeping in? Is the world with you or against you? You know how this works. Give yourself an honest mark out of 10 for how positive you are and mark it on the Positive Attitude spoke of your wheel.

Confidence

Do you lack self-confidence? Are you a shrinking violet who worries too much? Or are you full of certainty with high self-esteem? Most people believe they lack self-confidence but how much does it affect you? Give yourself a mark.

Motivation

Are you full of energy, highly motivated, jumping out of bed each morning with a spring in your step and the desire to get things done? It's a highly motivated high mark for you. Or is that snooze button just too inviting? Do you find yourself procrastinating? 'I'll do it tomorrow.' Then it's a low mark for motivation for you.

Open to change

The ability to be open to and accept change is a key to positive personal development. Everyone is happy to change the things they want to change, but what about when change is forced on you? How good are you at accepting change? And how well can you adapt? High marks for chameleons here!

Courses

So let's move on to what you are doing to improve your personal development, starting with your personal education. Here's a question: when was the last time you went on a course or seminar to learn more for your own development? And more importantly, did you pay for it yourself? If you're investing in yourself and devoting time to your personal development then it's high marks here, if you're not ...

Reading

Are you a bookworm, devouring books like this one to give you an edge? Or is your reading confined to the back of a cornflakes box? The fact you are reading this book right now gives you a couple of bonus marks (well done) but could you be doing more? Do you read books that only entertain or do you read books that make you better?

Keeping a journal

How do you know how well you are doing? Are you able to refer back two years and see what you were doing this week? Are you keeping organised references to the actions you are taking so you can refer back later and plot your journey? This one's easy: if you keep a detailed journal you get high marks; if you don't keep one at all – no marks. Sporadic journal writers get sporadic mid-range marks.

Mentors

Having a mentor (or two) is one of the best ways to keep yourself on track and move you to the next level of your personal development. If you have a formal mentor or coach, then well done – you'll be familiar with the benefits and you can give yourself a high mark. If, on the flip side, your mentoring tends to be asking a few friends in the pub 'what do you think?', then it's low marks I'm afraid.

So, now you have completed your Personal Development Wheel, join up your marks and take massive action by reading the chapters you need to focus on right now.

53

POSITIVE ATTITUDE

You must have heard it a million times. It's probably one of the key phrases associated with personal development: 'positive thinking'. But what does it mean?

When Napoleon Hill, who is credited as one of the main founders of the modern personal development movement, wrote *Think and Grow Rich*, he repeatedly used an expression that has stuck with me (and I'm sure with many others). He said, 'Thoughts are things.' The implication of this is that anything we have, or do, started with a thought. If that's the case, wouldn't it make sense that if you wanted to have positive things happen you should have positive thoughts?

Being negative is easier than being positive

Looking at the negative takes less creativity than looking for a positive. Having a moan is easier than being upbeat. Complaining seems more natural than complimenting. So, if you want to be different it will take some effort. Are you up for that challenge? I thought so; here's how.

Upgrade from just 'positive thinking' to taking 'positive action'

If you wanted to become a fitter person and you spent an hour each day thinking about it, how much fitter would you expect to become? Well, amazingly, some research suggests even by *thinking* about taking exercise you can become fitter (but only slightly). What if you spent that same hour going out for a walk, jogging, cycling, swimming or in the gym? I'm sure you'll agree your fitness levels would soar!

It's the actions that make the difference. Once I realised this I began to study actions and more specifically which positive actions would have the biggest effects. And I believe I found the answer by studying language and in particular, 'stimulus responses'. These responses occur at a subconscious level. Just as loud noises make us jump, we automatically use particular patterns of words to respond without thinking about what we say.

Choose your words carefully

I believe the foundation to changing your levels of positivity is your language. With over a million words to choose from in the English language and billions of others around the world, there has to be a more positive way to express how you are feeling. Here are some thoughts:

★ 'I'm sad' becomes 'I could feel happier' or 'I need to cheer up'.

★ 'That's useless' can be transformed to 'I think that could work better'.

★ 'I'm bored' becomes 'I need to make this more interesting'.

Take a few minutes to jot down five key negative words or phrases you use and see if you can change the words to express the same feeling, but asking for a positive result.

Here's the classic ...:

QUESTION: *'How are you today?'*

ANSWER: *'Not bad'* or *'Fine'*

I don't think many people carefully consider their response to that common question about their well-being. If, as Napoleon Hill suggests, thoughts are things, what sort of day would you have if whenever you are asked how you're doing you replied: 'Not bad.' Do you think that response would encourage your subconscious to create an amazing, creative, fun-filled adventurous day? Probably not. It's more likely you'd drift through another uneventful day, one pretty much like the last.

What if you changed your response and used a word like 'Brilliant!' Think about it. If you've been a 'not bad' person for years and you suddenly shock your brain by saying you're 'brilliant', what kind of subconscious actions are going to take place to fulfil this new belief about yourself? Brilliant ones!

I've been teaching people this simple method for change for over 15 years and the results are amazing. First, you feel better. Second, the person who asked you feels better. Third, it only takes 30 days for a 'brilliant' response to become a habit and then you'll always feel better.

OK, it doesn't need to be 'brilliant'; you may decide to have a different positive stimulus response for each day of the week:

Marvellous – Monday

Terrific – Tuesday

Wonderful – Wednesday

Tremendous – Thursday

Fabulous – Friday

Stunning – Saturday

Splendid – Sunday

Here's a challenge for you – test this one idea for the rest of today and measure the results.

Make a positive choice

The ability to choose how we feel or react to a situation is one of the most amazing gifts we have as humans. Most other animals can only respond – we can *reason*. The tragedy is, too often we don't.

My favourite movie is *The Castle*. It's an Australian comedy about a family who face the threat of a compulsory purchase of their home (their castle) because the authorities are planning to extend the local airport.

The opening scene features a monologue by the youngest son, Dale, as he describes the family home and each member of the family. If there was ever a brilliant example of positive choice, it's in this young man's description of their life. Most people would think that living bang next to an airport would be a pretty horrendous experience, but Dale's view is that it's just very convenient, should they ever need to fly somewhere – one day.

You may argue that the family are incredibly naïve; sorry, could be brighter. But the fact is they choose to see the positive in every situation. What better choices could you make?

Practise making these simple choices every day until they become part of a new and more positive you.

Making better choices

If you are caught up in traffic, could you see that as an opportunity to practise some breathing exercises? It's healthier; you can't control the traffic but can help yourself to live longer.

When it rains, do you choose to think about the green and pleasant land we live in or are you upset about the temporary inconvenience?

If something doesn't go your way, could it be that there's something bigger and better for you around the corner?

When something goes wrong, do you beat your chest and pull out your hair or take a step back and think: 'Now, what have I learned?'

BRILL BIT

Start to be positive with the weather. You can't control it, so, no matter what it does, look for the positives. Rain, wind, sun and snow, you name it. Find a reason to be thrilled and make the most of it.

54

CONFIDENCE

You could be the most qualified, well-organised, pleasant, polite person who appears complete in every way, but without the confidence to express who you really are, to share your ideas, to get people on board, then you'll always feel vulnerable.

Confidence is king!

When you meet someone who seems to ooze confidence, do you find yourself thinking, 'How lucky'? Guess what? Self-confidence is far from luck. You aren't born with confidence, it's a *learnt* behaviour. True, most confidence building is learnt during childhood but that doesn't mean you can't learn how to be more confident now.

Take this confidence test and score yourself out of 10 for each statement:

★ I find it easy to start a conversation with strangers.
★ I am happy to talk to strangers if they start to talk to me first.
★ I never worry about what people think about me.
★ I enjoy public speaking.
★ I make friends easily.

Total

Total up your score and see where you are.

★ **40–50:** You could write this chapter! You know the secret of self-confidence so I guess you are here to brush up a little.

★ **25–39:** Reasonable but I bet you'd rather do pretty much anything other than the public speaking!

★ **10–24:** I'm guessing you are confident with the 'known'. I predict you gave yourself a high mark for being happy to talk to a stranger who talks to you but not so high if you have to start the conversation yourself.

★ **0–10:** Oh, dear! Well, the good news is you can only become *more* confident! Let's start with a few tips.

Seven ways to guarantee an increase in confidence in just seven days

1 Think about what you are frightened of and overcome that fear first. By taking some time to identify what it is (specifically), you'll start to rationalise the thinking that takes place behind the fear. So, if you are worried about speaking in public then identify what it is about this worry. Do you fear it may all go wrong, that people won't listen, that you'll go bright red? Be as specific as you can be.

2 Master positive mental rehearsal. You have probably mastered the negative version already where you play images of the unconfident you. Instead, focus on playing an image where you look, feel and act confidently. Feel the fears but also see yourself overcoming them.

3 Baby steps. Take some small actions which reinforce your new confident self. Go to a different shop. Buy different food. Call a friend whom you haven't talked to for a while. Make eye contact.

Every time you take these actions, you reinforce in a small way that you are becoming more and more confident, so congratulate yourself.

4 Spend time with pleasant, confident people. I know it's difficult when you feel you are lacking confidence yourself, but it rubs off. I said pleasant people very deliberately. I mean confident people who will introduce you to others and who will look out for you. There's a thin line between confidence and arrogance and you want to spend time with the confident ones.

5 Tell yourself you are confident – but say it like you mean it. Affirmations are powerful tools to help you become more like the person you want to be. It's simple. If you want be more confident, start saying: 'I feel more and more confident, in every way, every day.'

6 'Act as if'. My friend Simon Woodroffe is the founder of YO! Sushi. When he first started in the restaurant business he'd be the first to tell you he had no idea how to run that kind of business. He needed backers, premises, partners and suppliers to make his new venture fly and he was terrified. His solution was to simply 'Act as if'. He would have meetings with suppliers and act as if he knew what they would need. He would present to banks and act as if he already had the money but he was just auditioning them for a little more.

When you 'Act as if', you quickly find yourself becoming that confident person.

7 Your lack of confidence is a learned behaviour. You weren't born with a lack of confidence; this means you must have learned it through life's experiences and usually the knocks that go with it. The good news is that because you've learned them – you can unlearn them. But here's a tip. When you unlearn something (take it out of your life) you must replace it with something positive. Lot's of people give up smoking but replace it with chocolate. Then they blame quitting smoking with getting fat! As you start to eliminate the worries and remove your limiting beliefs you must replace them with lots of positive new tools and techniques. You'll find them on every page of this book.

Confidence is a huge issue for most people and perhaps you can be reassured by the fact that you're expected to be totally confident in every area of your life. At the same time I'm sure a little more confidence would be welcome in your life. Some extra points scored here will have a positive effect on every other part of your Wheel Of Life.

BRILL BIT

There is only 'right' in learning.
      Often we worry we are going to 'get it wrong', which leads to low levels of confidence. If you change your thinking from 'right or wrong' to 'right or learning' then you'll only ever be right or learning.

MOTIVATION

There was once an old farmer in America's Deep South who struggled every day to make ends meet. When the oil companies started to drill for oil in the communities surrounding his land, he was approached but refused them permission to drill. He didn't want his neighbours and fellow farmers to consider him desperate and willing to give up his core business for the chance of a quick return. However, the oil companies kept asking him and, eventually, after a particularly bad harvest, he agreed. The test drilling gave good results so they bored a hole and set up a well, which was known as *Spindletop*.

Apparently, when you strike oil, it can blow the top off the 'derrick'. When *Spindletop* struck oil it destroyed the derrick. At that time it was the biggest oil find in American history. The farmer became a multimillionaire.

Here's the message. The farmer was already a multimillionaire. He had been walking across millions of dollars of assets. His father had been walking across millions of dollars worth of assets. The difference came about when the farmer was persuaded to take action.

So do *you* have a *Spindletop*? What success story lies beneath you just waiting to be drilled and taken to market? What are you missing because you can't get out of bed early enough or drag yourself away from the TV?

If you think 'If I knew I had a *Spindletop*, then I'd find all the motivation I needed to get to work', you'd be correct and you'd flourish right up to the first challenge; and then what would happen?

People who are motivated find a way; they get things done and they create energy.

So what stops you from getting motivated and what can you do about it?

Lack of energy

One of the primary reasons people lack motivation is they believe they don't have the energy. Now, notice I said they 'believe' they don't have the energy. Your body is amazing; it stores energy, so even when you think you are tired there's still loads of energy in reserve. The key is that, when you think you can't, change it to 'I must', then physically move your body. Give your fingers a wiggle, give your feet a shake, stand up and move about!

Fear of failure

Many people lack motivation because they fear they will fail, so they just don't bother to get started. Of course, that means they have failed – but once that cycle has started, it's hard to break. Unfortunately, the common perception nowadays is that it isn't good to fail. I think failing is so much better than not having a go, so go for it. Make it your mission to fail at three big things this week. I bet you can't.

Nothing to be motivated for

When I was a youth worker I was asked this question: 'Why do kids hang out on street corners?' My answer threw the questioner a little: 'Because hanging out on street corners is excellent, that's why.'

I'm sure he wanted me to go into some long explanation about how the youth of today are dysfunctional and how there should be 'more for young people to do'. But the point is unless the 'more for young people to do' is going to be more fun than hanging around the streets, they just aren't going to do it.

When I was 15 it was challenging at times to get me out of bed to go to school. Then an interesting thing happened – I fell in love. Well, I got a girlfriend, then suddenly I was out of bed at 7 am; in the shower; brushing my teeth for 20 minutes and getting to school early! I had suddenly found my 'why?'

Find your 'why?'

The real key to motivation is to find a big enough 'why?' and the rest will follow. To find your 'why?' see if you can work out what it is that motivates you.

Here's a list to get you started:

Recognition	Being the best	Money
Freedom	Fame	Revenge
The good things in life	Travel	Best quality
Being able to say 'It's done'		

With a big enough 'why?' the 'how?' becomes easier and with that you'll feel your levels of motivation start to increase. As always, the secret isn't in the knowing, it's in the doing.

BRILL BIT

If you still need to find your 'why?' write the words 'what's my big "why?"' in a note pad and leave it next to your bed. You'll be amazed at the dreams you'll have and the answers you'll wake up with.

56

OPEN TO CHANGE

If you were a sailor, you wouldn't complain if the wind changed direction, you would just reset your sails. So why is there so much fuss when we need to change? Some people really love change; my friend Llew Avis says: 'Every three years you should change your job, your home or your wife.' But the reality is that most of us fear it.

I live in Northumberland, right on Hadrian's Wall. I often marvel at the amazing technology the Romans brought when their empire came north. I also find it staggering that after they left we managed to go so far backwards before taking hundreds of years to catch up. You can imagine the scene after the last Roman left, with the locals saying: 'Thank goodness they've gone, now we can rip up those roads, destroy those ghastly sewers and get things back to how they used to be.'

We don't like change – even good change – if it is forced on us.

Learn to deal with it

When we are faced with change we often perceive it as a 'threat' and as such react with a 'fight or flight' response. In simple terms, we get very annoyed and either want to attack or run away. You can reprogramme your brain during these situations by learning how to use effective reasoning. One of the best ways to do this is through learning effective reasoning questions.

Imagine you are faced with a major change situation in your life; by asking these five questions you will definitely be equipped to deal with the change far more effectively:

1 Why has this change taken place?

2 What are the possible long-term positive benefits of this change?

3 What are the possible short-term benefits?

4 What can I do now to cope better with this change?

5 What can I do to benefit from this change?

You can't stop change, but you can adapt to it and even influence it

In the world of personal development, you can read many books and listen to many speakers saying how important it is to embrace change. This is all well and good when the change concerns the parts of your life that you want to change, but often this is not the case.

Some people deal with change better than others. This is often demonstrated by those who are either in, or would like to be in, the public eye. Just take a look at some newspaper headlines and spot a bit of 'positive spin':

Headline

Football star signs to new club and says he can't wait to play for such an amazing team

Reality

Footballer sold by old team because he's lost his form and he really wants the new club's fans to give him a chance

Headline

Local business lands £1 million contract

Reality

We're somewhat stunned to have pulled this one off, and actually in a bit of a panic as to how we're going to resource it!

Headline

TV star takes a year out to write movie script

Reality

No one wants to hire me so I'd better be seen to be doing something

What headline could you write to put a positive spin on the changes that are being thrust on *you*?

Headline

Tom makes dramatic new career move

Reality

Tom's been made redundant as his local office closes down

Headline

Sue reinvents herself with bold new image

Reality

Sue's boyfriend has dumped her and she could feel a whole lot better

If change is inevitable, why not be the person who is influencing the changes? It's a big step, but anyone can do it. From the smallest first steps to a major new direction, why not lead the way?

BRILL BIT

When faced with change play 'remember when'. Think about how things are now (particularly things that you accept), which, when they were first introduced, seemed to create major traumatic change.

57

COURSES

One of the best ways to develop yourself is to go for *total immersion*. You can do this in many ways but perhaps the very best way is by signing up to a personal development training course. I mean that in the widest context of personal development.

I left school with one 'O' level, in art. Not my proudest achievement. I wanted to leave and start to work. After a few years of working life I decided it might be fun to go to college and do an evening class in maths. I'd always enjoyed maths so spending a couple of hours on a Wednesday evening studying GCSE maths seemed like a cinch. And it was. This was closely followed by GCSE English and 'A' level psychology. I loved it! You could do a GCSE in one year instead of two. But the real beauty was that I was learning because I wanted to.

Later in life I discovered personal development courses. I remember an old boss of mine giving me some tapes to listen to on holiday. After a few days relaxing I put the first tape on and was transfixed by the content. When I went back to work my boss suggested we should go on the presenter's two-day course. Excellent, I thought, an all-expenses- paid business trip. I couldn't believe it when he said that if I wanted to go I would have to pay for it myself – I was furious. It turned out to be one of the best lessons I'd ever receive. Because I'd paid for it I was totally engaged; I wrote masses of notes and tested out every idea I learned.

I still go on lots of courses and I discover something new every time I take the opportunity to learn.

How do you find the right course (or courses) for you?

1 What do you want to learn? Note this is what *you* want to learn. This is not professional development; it's personal. There will be plenty of opportunities for you to attend multiple courses as part of your work. They are usually the ones you must attend, are paid for by work and are so mind-numbingly boring you can't wait to get to the bar. My question to you is: what do you really want to learn about? What's missing from your life or what are you passionate or even curious about?

2 A good first stop is your local further education college. There has never been a wider choice of courses to enrol for and don't think that you have to wait until September for the start of an academic year. Colleges are starting new programmes throughout the year.

3 If you are looking for a personal development course, take some time to narrow down the subject you are interested in. Personal development is vast and covers many topics. Are you looking for something to build confidence? Something to help you lead? What about relationships? Finance? Or your physical or spiritual self?

4 Can you commit? If you are signing up for a one- or two-day (immersion) programme that's easier than committing to three hours every Thursday evening to study Spanish. The challenge is, if you don't have the commitment and you miss a couple of weeks, then it's easy to quit.

So let's assume you've found a course (or two) to help you with your personal development.

At the time of writing this chapter, I have presented personal development programmes to well over a quarter of a million people. I've seen people change their lives in an afternoon and I've seen people walk out of a week-long programme barely touched by what they have experienced. How can you get the most out of a course or event?

How to get the most out of a personal development course

★ *Pre-read as much as you can.* Even though the presenter may be teaching exactly the same materials, being 'pre-read' helps you to digest the course materials at a deeper level.

★ *Get there early.* There is no excuse for being late and you will feel uncomfortable from the off if you arrive after the start.

★ *Sit as close to the front as you can.* This should be easy, as everyone wants to sit at the back. It's a brilliant affirmation that you are there to learn. This has only backfired on me once when I was a fundraiser and travelled to London for a course on 'large gift fundraising'. I sat at the front of a long thin room and was by myself until five minutes before the event started. I was then joined by a nice bloke who sat in the seat next to mine.

I opened the conversation with: *'Do you know why we are sitting here, right at the front?'*

'No', he replied. *'Why?'*

'It's an affirmation that we are here to learn. People who choose to sit near the front tell their subconscious mind that they want the information, so I believe they take more in.'

'That's brilliant, I agree with that', he concurred, before the host stood up to introduce the day.

He began by explaining who was going to be speaking and the timings. Then with a glint in his eye, he added: *'But before we start the official agenda, I am delighted to announce that we have one of the UK's leading philanthropists with us today who is going to share with you why and how he gives away over £750,000 a year.'*

By now my fundraiser instincts had taken over and I was frantically scanning the stage looking along the speakers table trying to work out which one was this hot shot donor giving away all this lovely money. I knew that, having sat in the front row, I'd be first to get to him during the break.

'So please give a big welcome to Mr Braun.'

As the crowd started to clap I turned to my new front row friend, winked and said: *'That's what we're here for, to get a lump of his cash, eh?'*

That was when he stood up, looked at me in a quizzical way and said: *'Are you now?'*, before walking to the podium to make his address.

So, as a word of warning, sometimes the speakers sit in the front row, too!

★ *Take lots of notes* and *learn like a teacher*. Taking notes improves your ability to recall information, even if you never read the notes again. I believe when you learn as a teacher (with the assumption that you need to teach others what you have learned), you learn more.

★ *Play full out*. A course is the perfect time to really go for it. You are in a safe environment; you are supposed to make mistakes! By stretching yourself on a course, it's easier to put those new ideas into practice in the 'real world'.

★ *Meet new people*. It always surprises me when people who already know each other spend all their time together at a course. You can learn masses and make amazing contacts during the breaks if you take the opportunity to mix with new people.

★ *Read your notes* at least twice after the course. The first time in the 24 hours immediately after the course and then once again in the next seven days.

★ *Take massive action* on what you have learned.

★ *Ask questions*. If you don't fully understand something and you ask a question, you'll become a hero because you'll have probably asked something that everyone else was thinking.

Attending a personal development training course will be one of the most rewarding experiences of your life. *I guarantee* if you find the right programme for you, every penny you invest will be repaid over and over.

BRILL BIT

Hands up if you have been totally inspired by what you have learned on a course, then promptly stuck your notes in the second drawer down, never to view them again?

Find one thing you can do immediately after a course to start your momentum towards taking massive action.

58

READING

Have you ever taught someone how to read? It's amazing how a mind starts to put together letters, shapes and sounds before making them into words. When you are teaching someone (usually the very young) how to read it's incredible when they first start to 'get it'. So once we've 'got it', when and why do we start to lose it?

Your ability to read is one of the most amazing gifts you have. However, in many cases, it's also one of the most underused gifts. The challenge is that we have so much to read just to get through our days, by the time we have a moment to ourselves can we really be bothered?

I was very fortunate to be introduced to a remarkable man called David Brown, who challenged me with a life-changing question: 'What are you doing right now for your own personal development?' It was one of those incredible turning points in my life. I asked: 'What should I do first?' He answered: 'Read.'

David Brown went on to explain that you can gather a person's life's work in a book. It may only take you a few days to read what it has taken them a lifetime to learn. The book you are reading now has taken me two years from the original idea to completion and you can read it over a weekend.

Reading is amazing!

Then the next stage is to get you hooked on reading and, as this is the personal development section, I suggest you begin by reading some books that will make you better.

How to Have a Brilliant Life is designed as an 'easy read'. Short chapters, lots of 'how tos', punchy lists and dozens of ideas for you to use immediately. I'm guessing that its simplicity is one of the reasons you picked it up. So find other similar books: Richard Templar's fabulous '*Rules of . . .*' books would be an excellent place to start.

I'm often asked for recommendations on what to read. We have a page on **www.michaelheppell.com** that simply lists books I've recently read and would recommend. Check it out or take a look at my publisher's website **www.pearsoned.co.uk/bookshop** for dozens of suggestions.

Who do you admire?

Perhaps one of the best and most interesting ways to improve your personal development through reading is to read biographies and autobiographies of people you admire. A word of warning: autobiographies tend to tell you how wonderful a person is (maybe because it is written by them?) and biographies tend to go for a 'warts and all' approach. There will be parts in both that you can take with a pinch of salt.

Trade press and specialist publications

There must be a magazine for every subject on the planet from *The Teapot Collector* to *World of Maggots Monthly*. I'm sometimes found open-mouthed in newsagents thinking, 'Who buys these?'

As you begin to read more, you may feel the need for more variety. What could you pick up to stimulate your brain?

Reading from the web

The biggest reading and research resource on the planet is known as the world wide web. The challenge is that 99.999% is of no interest to you whatsoever. So, you ask a search engine to help you. I remember many years ago that a search engine was described to me with this delightful metaphor: 'It's like a librarian who has a vast knowledge of the books on every shelf. When you ask them for a book they'll take you, in less than a second, and show you every book on that subject.' What a lovely description. What they didn't tell me was that the librarian is often happy to take a 'bung' for recommending one book over another and the content can range from brilliant to abysmal in a click.

The 'read' file

One of the challenges of being busy is finding the time to read articles, letters, features and the general 'stuff' that comes into our lives. I have a clear plastic file with the word 'READ' printed on the front. Anything I'd like to find time to read gets ripped out and popped into that file. When I find myself with some time in hand, usually at an airport or on a train, I take out my 'READ file' and work through the contents.

How to read and get the most out of reading a personal development book

★ Buy books, don't borrow them. Books are great value and, as you'll see, to get the most out of a book you need to personalise it.

★ Read the book with a highlighter and pen in hand. Highlight the paragraphs and sentences that have the biggest impact. Write notes in the margins.

★ Build your own library. You can build a library of hundreds of books over the years and give yourself an extraordinary reference collection.

★ Go back to favourite books. It's amazing what you see when you read a book twice. You could start with this one!

★ If you like a book, leave a small review on Amazon or other book websites. If you know you are going to review a book, you read it more carefully.

★ Share books you like by buying them for friends as gifts and saying: 'I loved this book, wanted to share it with someone I'm close to and I thought of you.'

★ Write to the author. If you like a book or if you want to find out more about their thinking, send them a note. You'll be surprised at how pleased authors are to receive your comments.

Write a book

One of the most common goals I hear is a person's desire to write a book of their own. If it's true that 'everyone has a book inside them', isn't it time you got yours out?

Book reading time. Most people read last thing at night. Here's a thought: why not schedule time to read for an hour in the morning or before dinner? You read in a different way and take more in.

59

KEEPING A JOURNAL

I'm a great 'futurist', but it's sometimes what has happened in your past that forms the type of person you will become in the future. As obvious as that may sound, just think about it. A lot of people spend their time living in the past, thinking about how things were. Some people spend all their time living in the future, not learning from their current experiences. The secret has to be to learn how to do both.

When you keep a journal it's a demonstration of your 'interpersonal intelligence'; this type of intelligence is the ability to know yourself. It's a very powerful intelligence and, by keeping a journal, it's one that can be learned.

Here's something for you to consider. Imagine it's 20 years from now. You're relaxing at home and you pick up your journal from 20 years ago. You read about the amazing year you had, the decisions you made and the people you met. You reminisce on the changes that seemed so big at the time and how you felt about the transformations taking place in your life. You realise that some of the decisions you made 20 years ago have culminated in the amazing life you lead now.

Let me share something with you. You don't have to wait 20 years. You could start to write a regular journal now and in just one year you'll be reading about this stage of life and it's fascinating. I'm writing this chapter in Ibiza now, and while my kids are reading Harry Potter I've brought some old journals to read while I'm not writing. Even after a few months, it's amazing to review your journal – I just can't recommend keeping a journal enough.

How to write a journal

1 Start now. Avoid the excuses of 'I'm too old' or 'it's too late'; do it now. Don't wait until Monday, the first day of a month or for something interesting to happen; just get started.

2 Invest in the best-quality note book you can afford. You are going to create a valuable asset, so make it look and feel special. Don't use a diary with dates preprinted on pages. Some days you may want to write a lot, others it will just be one line. Don't let your journal entry be limited by 'preprinted' pages.

3 Use a nice pen. It makes such a difference to your handwriting and it's easier to write more, too.

4 Write something every day. Even if it's just 'Monday 5th June. Feeling good but nothing much to write about today'. By getting into the habit of picking up and writing something in your journal every day it will stimulate you to add content.

5 Plan time to review your journal. I like to review mine at the end of each week, month and year. I also tend to look back at when projects, events and ideas started, to see how well I'm progressing and how different they are from my original thoughts.

6 Keep your journals safe. Journals often contain your most personal thoughts. Think about who you would or wouldn't want to have access to them and take the necessary action to protect your journals.

7 If you like using technology test out **www.ohlife.com**. It will remind you to write, give you snippets of old entries and virtually keep your information.

So what do you write?

You could write everything you have done that day or you could simply focus on the key elements of the last 24 hours. I decide, depending on how interesting my day has been and, as I write my journal last thing at night, how much energy I have.

As for the 'how?', you can do it pretty much any way you like but I would advise you to write everything of importance. Don't rely on your memory – it plays tricks over time. Capture your thoughts. Record meetings and introductions. It's nice to be able to go back to the first time you met someone and read your initial thoughts about them. Write your worries and fears and what you are excited about. Capture humorous moments – it's amazing to reread them. Document important conversations while they're fresh in your mind. Add drawings of places and people; they don't need to be works of art, but they'll help you relive a moment. Above all, be your authentic self. There is no more interesting a subject than you.

By keeping a journal you can refer back to different times in your life and read about your intriguing personal experience during those times. It's fascinating, like an opportunity to get a rerun of some of your favourite movies without having to pay for the DVD.

BRILL BIT

Add photographs and documents to your journal. With modern telephones and mini-cameras it's never been easier to capture moments of your life.

60

MENTORS

don't mean a mate whom you chat with now and then. I mean a person who will really push you, ask all the hard questions and educate you with specialist knowledge.

I'd always used mentors without actually realising it. I was one of those people who used to ask 'How do you do that?' to anyone I found interesting. When I was in my early twenties I was made a member of the British Youth Council. After the third meeting I attended I had a proposal I wanted to put to the council. Amazingly, it wasn't passed, but there were a record number of abstentions. I asked some other members why this had happened and the consensus seemed to be that I was a nice guy but when I stood up to speak most of the other members couldn't understand me. My strong North East accent was more powerful than my message!

I came home and immediately set about finding someone who could help me. Leonard Lonsdale was the answer. He was a local preacher whom I knew through my church and his voice was amazing. I called him and explained my dilemma. By the next day I had an elocution mentor who, although he couldn't teach me to speak like Prince Charles, did help me to become more easily understood and gave me bags of confidence.

Finding a mentor is easier than you think

★ Realise that you want to be better at something, then find someone who knows how to do it.

★ Ensure it's someone you admire and like. Your relationship won't work unless you highly respect, like and admire this person. You don't have to be friends or even know them personally.

★ Find a person who will push you. You don't need a mentor who will just tell you that you are doing a good job.

★ Don't chicken out! Once you decide on your amazing mentor don't put off asking them. We have all done it – thought about it then not taken any action.

★ Be clear with your request. Mentors will work with you so long as they know what is expected of them: two or three hours a month might be a good benchmark. Even if it doesn't take that amount of time, still communicate with them and be seen to use some of their knowledge. Even mentors go rusty!

★ Take a gift (but get creative!). The first time you meet your new mentor take them a small present. Make it memorable. Not tacky, not expensive, but make it something that will last.

★ Boost your mentor's confidence. Your new mentor could be as concerned as you are about taking on this challenge. Let them know specifically what you have learned at the end of each session and start your next one with what you have done and your results.

★ Make sure your mentoring is a one-way street. You aren't there to mentor your mentor. It may be that at some point you have an opportunity to become the mentor. I would suggest you park this opportunity at that moment and, at the end of your sessions, ask your mentor if you should switch roles.

Here's your homework. You have seven days to find a mentor. You don't need to have met with them but you must identify them. Ask them for help and have a first appointment scheduled.

Mentor groups

In Napoleon Hill's famous book *Think and Grow Rich*, he advocates surrounding yourself with a 'mastermind' group. A group of highly qualified individuals with specialist knowledge who would meet on a regular basis to help you. You may be very lucky and have a group of people able to do this. If you want to bring a new group together they may be thinking: 'What do I get out of this?' That's where mentor groups come in.

Mentor groups are a selection of like-minded people who come together and pool their knowledge for the benefit of each person in the group. By bringing a group together you can either get a real buzz or waste your time. I've helped several people establish these groups in the past and participated in a few, too. Here are the most common advantages, disadvantages and solutions.

Advantage: You have five or more people to give advice

Disadvantage: Five opinions that may clash

Solution: One person to chair each meeting whose ultimate say is final

Advantage: Conversation leads to unknown creative territory

Disadvantage: You don't actually get any advice transferred

Solution: Have three clear agenda items and a good chair who leads you back to them

Advantage: Mix of minds allows you to get several opinions on how to tackle an issue

Disadvantage: People who have little knowledge of your problem wanting to give their opinion

Solution: Think transferable. Accept all the advice that people give but think how you can adapt it more specifically to your situation

If you are thinking about setting up a mastermind mentoring group, keep in mind the following:

★ Be very clear with the people you are inviting and let them know what is expected of them. Tell them they will probably be doing more giving than getting. You need a group who are all happy with this mindset.

★ Suggest you are going to test it for three meetings (one a month) to see how it goes. Arrange the dates for all three now.

★ Ensure everyone gets something out of the first meeting.

★ Write to (don't email) everyone who attended the first session to thank them for their contribution.

★ Suggest that, after the first three meetings, if someone wants to leave they replace themselves with someone who would add to the group.

★ Keep it fast, fun and fresh. As soon as it becomes too much like hard work it's time to stop.

Having a mentor (or two) is one of the best ways to keep yourself on track and move you to the next level of your personal development.

You'll be amazed at how much people will want to help you if you ask in the correct way and be open to their suggestions.

It may be that as you read this you like the idea of being a mentor yourself. There are lots of ways to do this but one of the most rewarding is to work with young people. Ask your local secondary school if they have a mentoring programme. Many do and they are always looking for committed people who want to help.

BRILL BIT

Four brilliant words will ensure you get success when you ask someone to mentor you. They work in a magical way and you'll be amazed at the results when you use them. Quite simply they are: 'I need your help.'

FINAL NOTE

So that's it. You've completed *How to Have a Brilliant Life* but in many ways (and forgive me for the cliché) your journey has just begun.

Having a Brilliant Life isn't just about reading a book, it's a work in progress and for you it has well and truly started. Think about the challenges you were facing 10 years ago or even 10 days ago; they're different from the ones you're facing right now. That's why I want you to keep this book in hand and use it as a reference manual.

Complete your Wheel of Life once a month and check with the chapters where you need some help. Make it a must to do this. I have 'Wheel of Life' as an appointment with myself on the first day of every month. It's set up as a recurring item ensuring it will always be there, month on month, year on year. You can do the same – now.

My final message goes right back to where we started. If you've read this book cover to cover you will now be familiar with over 100 tools and techniques to help you in all areas of life. However, being aware of them is very different from putting them into action.

My challenge to you now is to use what you now know, test out the ideas, take some chances, don't settle for second best, create a new benchmark – and above all have a Brilliant Life!

RECEIVE 90 DAYS
OF BRILLIANCE PLUS SOME
POWERFUL FREE BONUSES

If you have enjoyed *How to Have a Brilliant Life* and you would like more resources to help you on your quest for brilliance, including:

★ bonus chapters

★ '90 Days' – our special 12 week personal development programme

★ a regular newsletter packed with motivation, hints and tips

then take action and visit **www.michaelheppell.com** now and sign up for our free newsletter.

Tell us you've read *How to Be Brilliant* and we'll send you these extra goodies too.